REALLY MOVING ON

HEALTHY WAYS TO LET GO AND FIND CLOSURE

Cover Design: Will Morris and Patti Jefferson
Editor: Carla DuPont

ISBN-13: 978-1-949191-16-5

For more information, please visit:
pierrejeanty.com

Schools & Businesses

Jeanius Publishing books are available at quantity discounts with bulk purchases.
For more information, please email
contact@jeaniuspublishing.com

Contents

DISCLAIMER

The purpose of this book, or of any of my relationship books, is to guide you, help you gain new perspectives, and sometimes further confirm you are already making the right choices. This book was written to help motivate you to make wiser choices, better decisions, and find the light at the end of the tunnel.

For many, this will help you assess your relationship as a means to understanding it and equip you to overcome it. The thing about heartbreak, or any relationship topic, is that sometimes our emotions cloud our judgement; they keep us from doing what needs to be done until a voice other than ours or one we are familiar with comes into the picture.

We must be clear about one thing before we move forward, this book will not take away the difficulties, temptations, reality, or fill in the gap where you should be applying willpower, executing or practicing self-control.

Growing and healing takes real work, real effort, and consistency amongst other things. However, it will help make things easier, help you fight the temptations, embrace and deal with reality, while giving you confidence to take control and do as you need to.

The focus of my heart is to help you navigate; but, I can't do the walking, swimming, or driving for you. I can never replace the obstacles that must be overcome. I can only give you better directions to overcome them.

REALLY MOVING ON

HEALTHY WAYS TO LET GO AND FIND CLOSURE

INTRODUCTION

The relationship you thought was going to last came to an end. Maybe you saw it coming, maybe you didn't. Maybe you were tired of trying to keep something dead, alive, and finally decided enough is enough. Maybe you were on the other end where you were the partner they needed to move on from. Whatever reason led to the separation, whatever corner you're on, the fact still remains that it hurts.

Breaking up is hard; it's devastating. The heartache isn't getting any better and you want a cure for it. Something to help ease the pain, to help let go of the pain, to find the smiles, the happiness, the belief in love again. Even though I am happily married, I can still remember my last heartbreak. I remember feeling sick to my stomach. I couldn't stop thinking about what was and how it would no longer be. I remember how much sadness took the wind out of me and I became hopeless. All I wanted at that time was for the hurt to cease, the memories to vanish, and hope to come back to me. I remember thinking love wasn't for me. How could it be if I kept getting it wrong? It kept running away from me. Heartbreak seemed easier to find than lasting love.

It's painful, I know that far too well. Even when you can see the end of the relationship being near, when it happens, it's still hard. It's funny how easily you come together like magnets; yet, coming apart is as hard as trying to force opposite ends of those same magnets together. They were once part of your life, removing them and trying to move forward is a process you will have to go through. It will not be an easy process; it will take some tears, discipline, and hard work. There's light at the end of the tunnel, as long you are walking your way out.

Before you dive into this book, I want to commend you for taking this step. This book being in your hands right now tells me you are serious about picking up the pieces. You are doing what it takes to put that relationship in the past. This alone is growth. This is a step many people need to take, yet don't for whatever reason. Some are either too afraid or too insecure believing that they will not find love once they leave. Others are manipulated and sadly abused into staying, and so forth.

There are countless people stuck in terrible relationships, living like a hamster in a wheel, circling around hoping they will eventually find their way out. But don't. Better has never shown up and will not show up. The truth about better is that it will not just come, at least a better that will last.

It's like catching a fish. First, you have to equip yourself. You have to show up, lay the right bait, and apply patience. Better has to be found. I promise you, yours is on the way. The fact that it's over and you are looking to put the pieces of your heart back together, find your happiness outside of them, and move forward is beautiful. Give yourself a pat on the back, be easy on yourself. You are doing all you can do.

A reward will come with that. Your smiles will come back to you, your joy will be louder, your happiness will become more unshakable. This is a journey but there's a reward. The hard work pays off. Be proud you are focusing on putting the pieces together and laboring for your healing. Finding a better you after overcoming something many do not overcome properly is a gift you will cherish.

I'm proud of you, very proud of you. Now let's get to work.

1

Why you need to "REALLY MOVE ON"

When experiencing heartbreak, the answer to why you need to move on is obvious. Who wants to keep holding on to a relationship or a phase that is no longer fruitful? Who wants to carry the pain of heartbreak like a trophy? No one, that is. You want to move on because you have to, because not doing so is robbing you of your happiness, peace, love. It's blinding you from too many good things waiting on you. It's simply a fire that needs to be put out.

If those things that come with moving on are enough, why do you need to "REALLY MOVE ON"? Because the fire being put out is oftentimes not enough. It's foolish to have your house burn down, put in the work to repair it, and not put in safety measures to make sure it doesn't happen again or at least the same way. There should be measures to keep the heartbreak from coming easily again. There should be more effort into making sure the same destruction doesn't target your heart or at least better preparation to put a similar fire out quicker or even recognize what is beginning quicker.

There's truly a difference between moving on and *really* moving on. The difference determines whether you endure this or overcome it. Moving on is the first phase for anyone who has had their relationship end and forward is their focus. The goal is to get to the other side of it all. It takes a lot of work but it's still level one, which many do not realize. You no longer think about them, are no longer emotionally attached to them, you're no longer practicing habits that revolve around them. That's the first phase.

It's important; as life changing as any other phase but there's more to it. It's not about good versus bad here, it's about good versus great. Getting past the first phase of your healing is good. Well, what's next? Taking the lessons and applying them how they need to be applied, using experience as a tool for growth. Preparing your heart for the next person, or simply for love. Not allowing this past you are leaving behind to alter how you perceive love or cause you to be blind to something true.

Really moving on is going deeper, it's focusing on the residue, making sure that leaves as well. It's analyzing the experience, using the lessons to not only put them in the past but become more prepared for the future. Really moving on is about making sure you're over them, as well as not unknowingly letting the experience change you however it pleases. It's controlling how you change and why you change. It's taking the wheels and choosing which direction you go.

Why do you need to really move on? Because everything we experience shapes us. The relationship, the heartbreak, and the mess after are seeds that have been planted and can eventually grow in your soul. You must make sure they bear fruits instead of becoming cancer haunting your next love life. There are so many people out there who've moved on; yet, unknowingly become the person who hurt them to the new partner in their next relationship. The term 'hurt people hurt people' lives because people think just moving on from the situation is enough. That's settling for the minimum. The smart thing to do is to get the maximum result from this situation. To make sure there are no unresolved issues holding you back.

The Right
Understanding

With the right understanding, you begin to take the right steps to move forward.

Without it, you will only find yourself taking steps that lead nowhere or in the wrong direction.

The difference between letting go and moving on.

Are you trying to let go? Or are you trying to move on? Don't answer the question yet. Once we get deeper into the book, you will have the opportunity to ask yourself again and answer honestly. Right now, our focus is understanding the difference and why it's important. If we are honest here, the two terms are clear about their directive, they are both leading to do different things. Yet, many believe they are one and the same.

The truth is, they are not. There's a gap between the two. Realizing the mistake people make when speaking on the two helped me frame the title of my book.

Letting go is releasing something, it's detaching yourself from something, it's freeing yourself from something you no longer want to be entangled with. Letting go is about separation, it's about ending the chapter.

Moving on, however, is about flipping the page. Moving on is moving away from what or who you are letting go of. It's more than just freeing yourself from something, it's making sure that something doesn't have access to you anymore, that it's not holding you back, it's not holding on to you and affecting your future. Moving on is about leaving the past behind and being better prepared for the future. The word 'move' is in the phrase for a reason, it's asking you to move from whatever you need to or have to let go of.

Both letting go and moving on are stages you must go through after suffering heartbreak. To successfully go through the stages, you must remember you cannot move on until you let go. Letting go is the first phase of this journey to a stronger and healed you, moving on is the second phase. One of the things that keeps people from really moving on besides not understanding the phases is not keeping the order. There are a lot of people trying to move on without letting go. They find themselves doing everything to forget their ex and put the relationship in the past without doing the work that needs to be done to let go. You cannot move away from something until you stop holding it. If you are holding a door, you cannot just walk away from it. You either find the strength to drag it with you or you loosen your grip, free your hands from it and start marching away from it.

Understanding the difference between letting go and moving on will grant you the opportunity to plan properly to reach your goal. How can you build something strong without a foundation? This is setting the foundation, laying down the stepping stone. Now that you are aware of the two phases, it's time to create your strategy to win, your roadmap to the end result you are searching for.

You can't do it alone.

One of the most vital things to understand about this journey is that you can't do it alone. It will require a lot from you, but you shouldn't carry it all by yourself. You will have to make sacrifices, endure, and persevere, among other things. The journey to becoming whole doesn't have to be a lonely road, a path traveled only by you.

When you are buried under the weight of memories, emotions, and disappointments, it'll be easy to feel and believe you are the only one going through this; the only one hurting, the only one who has been fooled. That is so far from the truth.

As I am writing this, at this very moment, thousands of people around the world are trying to deal with heartbreak just like you are; people who are trying to find closure, people who can't wait to close the door on their past relationships, yet can't seem to find a way. You are not alone, you are not the only one trying not to let the pain swallow you. I chose to write this book because there are more people like you.

As a poet, one of the things that helped me find success is how relatable many people found my writing to be. Many have said I've been able to say things they've always wanted to say but couldn't find the words. Or the way I've captured their feelings are so unique. When I send poems to my email club, often times we see replies that say, "OMG! You know exactly how I feel!"

The truth is, I don't know how they feel. I know how it felt when I was in that situation. I know what my friends and family members felt. And in some cases, how my life and relationship coaching clients felt when they were going through those times in their lives. I didn't put their feelings into words, I used mine, the things I know, I've observed, and even heard. That's the thing about heartbreak and pain, it shuts you down. It lies to you and tries its best to corner you and steal every bit of your attention.

When you are fighting for your smile, your laugh, your happiness, and your heart, it's easy to feel alone. Countless people feel alone even when they aren't going through these things in this forever connected world.

It's an absolute lie. A lie I am exposing right now.

After writing this book, I created a course that also comes with a community as a bonus feature. This is how serious I am about making sure readers like yourself see that you aren't alone. Recognizing that will give you and others a sense of relief. Feeling like you're the only one can create baggage even the biggest plane can't carry. Every bad thought, every bad day, every breakdown, someone out there in the sea of people is experiencing it as well. You are not alone. No one is truly alone.

This is a message that needs to be preached more often; lives are lost because of this. I've known people who ended their lives because pain cornered them and they didn't have the right help to confirm that they weren't alone.

I encourage you to join a community of people who are on this journey. At the least, surround yourself with people who understand what you're going through and who are there for you. The lie of "being alone" keeps us carrying weight we don't have to. You don't have to fight the pain alone. You aren't alone. You will never be alone.

It's not supposed to be easy.

When we get into a relationship, we start to invest ourselves, time, emotions, love, heart and, to some, our entire soul. How can pulling out ever be easy? How can it not be hard to detach yourself when you were so emotionally involved? It's never easy to have to detach yourself from someone you've joined yourself to, someone you grew to love, to know their habits, to memorize their laugh, to recognize the smallest details about them. You can't just remove someone whose been part of your days and nights so easily. This is someone you were intimate with, you worked on being with, you gave your soul to. It's like gluing your hands or any body parts together then trying to separate them. This will not be an easy task, free from burdens and consequences.

What I am getting across is that this journey of letting go and moving forward will not be easy. It will not seem easy. It takes work. You will feel like giving up sometimes. You will feel like running away from the things you need to do to heal properly. You must put one foot ahead of the other to keep on moving until you reach your goal. Nothing easy ever gives satisfactory results. You're fighting for something that will take time, courage, and won't come at the drop of a hat. It'll take getting smacked and pushed down by all sort of thoughts, opinions, feelings, and emotions. You may even find yourself back in their arms, running back into what you know even when you know it isn't good for you. There will be countless things you face trying to close this chapter. You must face them head-on and run through them instead of away from or around them.

The only time you'll hear the word 'easy' mentioned concerning heartbreak is from the mouths of people who aren't counting the cost of which they speak. People who can only imagine but not feel the weight of the current state you are in. It's vital that I mention this to you while telling you it's not going to be easy because some will subconsciously try to convince you that things being hard are because something is wrong with you. Those people will say things like, "You should move on...you deserve better...

time heals all wounds...let go and let God..." I'm sure you're familiar with the list of popular sayings floating around the internet.

They'll throw those bandage words, thinking they are problem solvers when you're trying to break free from a broken heart and put that relationship in the past. That's the advice of well-meaning people who aren't currently sitting with a shattered heart, trying to make sense of it all and find the best way heal.

It's easy to give the best directions to someone who is playing the game when you're just spectating. It's easy to give directions when you aren't the one who is lost. A wise man I know once said, "My stubbed toe, hurts me more than your gun shot." A weird proverb but the point stands. What you are going through hurts you more than anyone else's hurt right now despite the fact some are facing worse challenges.

The well-meaning people aren't in your shoes. They aren't fighting the emotional battles, you are. They aren't doing the crying, losing their appetite, feeling betrayed by that person right now. You are. They may have been there, but they aren't there right now. It's not real to them at this moment. It's painful, it's loud, it's consuming...to you. The last thing you need is advice that makes you feel like they are trying to silence your reality. Don't let their well-meaning words sit in your ears for too long.

I am saying this because I've been on both sides. I used to be one of those well-meaning people who soon realized that being detached from the pain makes it easy to say things. Things that, being on the other side, I realized were discouraging and misleading. I keep using the term 'well-meaning people' because a lot of people don't realize how detrimental their advice can be to your journey. Some just want you to know they've endured worse and survived. This is a way for some to tell you that you can do it because they've done it. Unfortunately, another group will tell you to suck it up, get over it. It's a way to softly tell you only weak people stay down like this. They are wrong. They aren't being realistic. They are brushing over real issues.

I hope I made it clear to you that it's not going to be close to being easy. It will help you approach this journey more prepared to go to war to pick up the pieces. There will be no misconceptions that the result you desire will come in without a strong fight. It'll be hard but you can do it.

Secondly, people will come with their opinions about your pain but you don't have to accept them. It's almost unpreventable, it's a norm in our society for people to speak with the mentality that this should be a quick sting, like it's a childish stage you are experiencing instead of a real-life thing you are dealing with. Some treated heartbreak that way which is why they haven't found healing themselves. Letting those opinions and that mindset settle in has helped too many people fall faster into denial and unhealthy coping methods to not warn you about them. You can't skip the process, part of it is going through the hurt.

I've been asked numerous times before, "How do I get over them? I don't want to feel this anymore." It's a natural reaction to want to run from the pain trying to find the easiest route out of your current reality. The entire first part of learning to move on properly is acknowledging the task at hand is one not easily achieved. Despite the pain, one must choose the best way to deal with it. It's there because what you had was a real-life event that takes real work.

Don't let people discredit the reality of it and you should choose not to run away from it. Let knowing that it's not easy become your fuel. Gear yourself up to fight for your joy, your smile, your happiness, and your love back.

It's not supposed to happen fast.

Understanding healing is not supposed to be easy, many also understand it's not supposed to be a speedy recovery type of deal. Unfortunately, when dealing with emotions and heartache, sometimes logic is the last thing that shows up to this process. Moving on will not happen fast, it's not supposed to; neither is it a race to move on before your ex.

Once a relationship is over, not only do we want the pain to be gone quickly, but we want to be over our partner as fast as possible. We want everything to just dissolve in a heartbeat, the attachment to be gone yesterday, the memories erased, and the feelings in the past. We want to put everything in our rearview mirror or operate with the mentality that it doesn't exist, even go so far as to wish the relationship didn't exist.

Just like we rush into most of the relationships we will need to heal from, we rush to the finish line with our moving on journey as well. Think about that for a second.

Rushing into relationships is the reason many people are dealing with heartbreak to start with. Yet they are trying to rush the process as if the last thing they rushed did not land them where they are.

Sadly, it's easier to push yourself to act healed before you are, to start doing things you aren't ready for, to start being with people you aren't ready to be with and even jump in relationships you have no business being in. The danger in moving fast is that it makes you feel like everything is okay when things are simply ignored and neglected. It gives you false results. It's vital for you to slow down and understand that your journey to moving on has to be a slow cooked meal, good for the soul rather than microwaved fast food there to satisfy your hunger quickly but only for a moment.

It's better to find closure and healing late than to never find it at all. Pretending they exist in your life where they don't, doesn't do any good at all. It only creates a weak foundation upon which better cannot be built. Take your time, pace yourself. Doing things right is more important than just doing them. Even when you are putting effort towards doing it the right way, (which you are by reading this book), you can still end up taking the wrong steps along the way by not giving everything its appropriate time to come into fruition. There's no real reward by rushing anything unless the reward is in coming first. The reward here is not for that, the reward is proper healing that will help you find your happiness again and even prepare you for your next relationship.

Also, to better pace yourself, you must understand that you are your own competition. An evolved version of you that learned from the relationship is who you are in competition with; the person who is in the mirror. It's the old you versus the new version of you, and no one else. Unfortunately, when you are trying to make things happen quickly, it's easy to lose sight of the real goal. This often leads to people treating this as a competition battle between themselves and their ex. It becomes all about who can move on faster, who can start doing better quicker, who is in more shape, looks happier, making more money... a list of silly comparisons that can only be measured on shallow levels.

This is what happens when you take your eyes off the prize, you stop looking in the mirror and stop moving at a pace that is right you. Your ex becomes a rival that shouldn't exist. You will find yourself distracted from the real goal. We've all heard comparison is the thief of joy. So, when you're trying to get your joy back, you must leave no room for comparison.

When you stop trying to beat your ex at a speed game that isn't supposed to exist, is when you start to lay the foundation to find joy quicker. This is another way people let the person who broke their heart continue to break it, by giving them a power or attention that they shouldn't be getting in the first place. It's important to know who the real enemy is here. It's not who hurt you anymore, it's you against you. You against the old you, the broken you, the hurt you. That enemy can't be fought, it has to be conquered.

Do not rush this process, do not make it about anything else. This is about you doing what you need to do to be you again. This is about you walking the long journey back to you, to a better you. This is about planting the right seeds and allowing them to grow roots so you can bear the fruits that are good for yourself. Pace yourself, stay in your lane, and get tunnel vision; that's how you reach your destination. It's never a race.

How to NOT move on?

There are right ways to move on and wrong ways to do it as well. If you're reading this, by now you've explored some of the wrong ways to do it. Obviously, they exist. Despite some people believing that as long you are doing something to move on you're good, the truth lives on the opposite of that. There's a right and wrong way to do almost everything and anything, recovering from heartbreak is included in that. There are countless things you can do to move on that will wreck you more than the failed relationship will. However, clinging to the wrong ways to get over an ex seems to work for many people. Why face everything head-on when you can run around it and leave it in the past? This is an illusion many get eaten up by the danger of. It's usually short lived because sooner or later, the band-aid placed on the problem will fall off and expose the untreated wounds.

There's always a shortcut to everything, often full of promises, easy, all reward and minor risk. Shortcuts only show fast rewards. Similar to a get rich quick scheme, the more you go down that path, the harder making a U-turn becomes. Not that it's impossible but when we don't want to put effort in doing things the way they need to be done, we put effort on the wrong ways which ultimately drains us. It also pushes us to be less motivated to do things the right way.

Now, let's dive into the wrong ways people move on.

You can't drink it away.

Someone once told me that heartbreak makes the best body builders. My response was, "The best poets and alcoholics, too." The emphasis here is on the alcoholics. One of the wrong ways people deal with heartbreaks that I've observed to be the most harming is abusing alcohol. Of course, there are situations that have caused more harm. Yet, nothing seems as consistently harmful to me. Neither is it talked about as often as a destructive coping method to the level it should be discussed. It's a silent but deadly force that is often underestimated. Being that drinking is socially acceptable and fits into so many people's lifestyles, abusing

REALLY MOVING ON   37

it can easily be missed, overlooked, or taken lightly.

When your heart is shattered, you have to deal with a hurt that can't be touched or treated with medicine to help with physical pain. The fact that it's an emotional and mental battle, it's easy to run to something that can numb it since there's no direct treatment for those things. It's easier to dive into something to help endure the reality, not fully evaluating if that 'something' is good, compared to a prescription a doctor may give you for physical pain.

To feel every ounce of your heartache's existence is unbearable sometimes. It hits people differently. To those who find it to be rock bottom in their life, it pushes them to run into something that can make the heartache feel like it's gone. It's the first thing many have on their agenda. They need something to make them forget all of what they are dealing with. Unfortunately, alcohol achieves that for many of those people. It's a perfect magic trick. The more you gulp it down, the more you press the ignore button. Alcohol gives such an opportunity to avoid reality so subtly that it can even be considered irresistible.

The best way I've been able to help some people see

the danger and why it's such a rewarding trick when you don't want to deal with this is by using this example. Let's say you go out to play baseball with a few friends. You get there and as you are walking on the field, the bat escapes someone's hands directly in front as they practice their swing. The bat flings in your direction and hits you right next to your temple. You fall unconscious immediately. The next thing that happens is you wake up in the hospital with a bandage on your head in some sort of pain; yet, you're ready to head home.

There's nothing good about being unconscious but there's definitely a benefit in this situation. Not having to feel the pain on your way to the hospital, see the blood, carry the worry while enduring the distance to the hospital and wait to be treated is a blessing.

Jumping right into the last part of this is something most people would prefer instead of being aware every step of this unfortunate event. Being unconscious has its perks when it comes to this situation. However, did you endure less force? Was the damage less severe? Will the aftermath be different? Nope it's the same attack, same pain, possibly different outcome. You being presented with a seemingly quicker solution, doesn't take anything away from you having some serious head damage that will need to heal properly.

This is the truth for abusing alcohol and even drugs, they provide people an opportunity to run from the pain all while not minimizing it but instead adding to it. Many people don't realize this. Numbing the pain or not experiencing it at every moment doesn't make the damage less or that there's less to heal from. It only means you're getting a temporary relief in this situation, a relief that happens to be another façade causing more pain and even threatening your well-being on a different level. Alcohol may provide an escape but it's adding more things you'll need to escape from.

You can't just go to the next.

When you're dealing with a broken heart, you will battle many things. In the long list of those things, loneliness will work its way right to the top. It's in our nature to have a desire for comfort, companionship, reassurance, physical touch, and truly everything that falls under the umbrella of love. Those things we can somewhat bring to ourselves, taking the self-love route or even draw them from our friends and family members on the platonic relationship level. However, romantic-less love will not be enough in most cases, if not all.

The need for companionship, comfort, attention, physical touch, and a romantic connection is almost unstoppable. There's no better time it will be evident to you that human beings aren't meant to live without relation-ships than during heartbreak. This is why people feel like they must respond to these cravings and find the next best person for them. People jump into the next person's arms because they have wants and needs. Why stay miserable and work on something as hard as healing and practice patience when you can find something that can give you what the last relationship didn't? The answer is simple here. Choose to be happy with someone else.

This is the thought process for many who failed to slow down and truly evaluate why they are running to the next relationship. They don't feel like it's them running

away but them running into something they'
looking for and could be in this next person.

If you're doing this now or have done it, like I have,
you know it's hard to see yourself actually running away
from dealing with the heartbreak. Instead, you see it as an
opportunity to be happy and in love again. I've been there.
It's easy to convince yourself that you simply missed it on
the last relationship and this one will be different. When
emotions are involved, desperation starts to scream at you
and you have burning desires; you can't help yourself
sometimes. Everything will feel right until the relationship
ends up being another wrong one.

Jumping from one relationship to another is like
drinking poison for medicine. Despite how you want it to be
something good, it will do its own internal destruction that
you will not realize until it's too late. It doubles almost
everything. Your heart will become shattered twice into
more pieces. Since the pieces before were never put
together, the pain will hurt twice as much. Trust issues hit
twice as hard, your belief in love will weaken more than it
did before. When you are heartbroken, another

relationship should be the last thing on your list despite what you think or feel. There will come a time when you will be able to walk into a new relationship. Right after you've walked out of one isn't the time. When you're bleeding and vulnerable is not the best time to find love.

Overcoming Emotions & Enduring Feelings

Without emotions and feelings, we are just robots; they make us human. How we process them, makes us better or worse as humans.

Validating your reality.

You cannot move on until you process, endure, and overcome the range of emotions and feelings you will go through on this journey. We will talk about some of the most important ones later in this section; but, it's crucial that we talk about the reality of them.

Emotions and feelings are almost unavoidable, they were needed to build the relationship, their presence will still be there even after the relationship. As a matter of fact, the emotional side of things will be half of the battle to get to your healing. You will feel a variety of things and go through many emotional stages as you aim to close this chapter in your life. The emotions and feelings will never be the problem, how you handle them determines how long you will be on this path and whether you truly heal or not.

In order to come out on top of the tough emotions and feelings instead of letting them drown you, it's important to understand they are validating your reality. They are doing nothing more than showing you that you are at a crucial stage requiring you to pay close attention to yourself and how you deal with them. This is also the stage where you must prioritize your mental health and stay very self-aware. Emotions having the ability to influence our decision making and feelings being able to influence how long we stay in our decisions, must be watched.

Besides them being powerful, they are also a great indicator that you are living. This is the focus of this section, to let you know that the different emotions you go through and feelings you experience, are a reminder that you are in a fight, that you are courageously trying to achieve something hard. Similar to a lifeline, us being in different emotional stages of feeling up and down is every proof that you are handling it instead of letting it guide itself. The inconsistency is more of a beautiful sign than most people realize. Emotions are meant to be temporary. They aren't meant to control our lives, we are meant to control them. When we don't, they develop into feelings and that's where the danger starts to creep in.

Let's say, while you are thinking about a few memories, you start to experience sadness. The sadness is an emotion, it happens instantly. Then, the feeling of sadness starts to take over. Many will let the feeling take over, controlling them longer than they are supposed to which leads to depression and all sort of other soul-sucking feelings. Here's the point. Someone who isn't doing what it takes to go forward will allow that emotion and feeling to take control and completely swallow them. The unfortunate thing is that it can go as far as robbing their life.

This is why emotions coming and going is a good sign. Being emotionally dormant shows lack of effort. You, on the other hand, are fighting against the wave. You are not allowing them to sit and overthrow what you need to do. The inconsistency that your emotions and feelings lay at your door is an important piece to this puzzle. It's proof that there's a fight in you, it's proof that you understand the battleground, it's proof that you are aware and using awareness is how you win.

I've met people who feel like they aren't moving or can't move on because of the inconsistency of their emotions. One day they think the best of their ex, see every reason they should be together and are willing to work it out. The next day, they hate their ex, wish the experience never existed and are just plain angry. As unbalanced as this may sound, it's a good sign. The waves aren't always violent or always calm; we know the sea is alive when both happens.

So, I beg you to see these ups and downs differently. They are good, they are a good indicator, they validate the reality of your current state. Don't let them become tools of discouragement. It's you going through it to get on top. Understanding this will help you learn how to overcome more than you realize.

Allow yourself to feel everything.

Our feelings aren't meant to rule us. We are supposed to live through the feelings. Letting your feelings pick which mood you will be in, the emotional state you will be in, and so on doesn't help you at all. Processing those feelings, however, is a crucial part of your healing. They are phases you are meant to experience to help purge everything out. It's crucial that you allow yourself to feel every stage of the heartbreak. Let the pain push you to cry if you need to, let the anger get screams out of you, let the fear come in and expose those thoughts that need to be conquered.

Feel everything without missing a step, even vent to people you can trust to keep your business private if you need to. Feel everything; this is how you purge yourself of it all. If you don't cry it out, you bottle up those emotions which can eventually be poured into the wrong places. If you hold the screams in, you eventually let them out on the wrong people and for the wrong reasons.

When the fears of not being good enough, worthy

enough, of not being able to love or be loved come without being processed, you hide them and let them become insecurities that eat away at the good things that come your way. When you don't vent, those thoughts sit in your mind, dwell and multiply which only make matters worse through overthinking.

Feel everything that comes your way, the sadness, the darkness, the crack of light that creeps in, the disappointment. Feel them all so they can be processed and flushed out of you. Overthinking alone is one of the silent killers that take people off track when trying to move on. Overthinking always finds the worst possibilities or routes, which ultimately take people down a sadder path.

When I faced my last break-up, I cried 'til I had no tears left. My friends even saw me cry. (This is not as common amongst guys as it is for women.) It was pretty clear to everyone when the crying didn't stop and I wasn't eating much. Eventually, I grew angry, thinking of the broken promises, their mistakes, the blame that person cast on me, and so forth. I let out random screams and devoted myself to running and working out to deal with it. I exercised, not to get in shape, but to show them I was looking better without them. (And I made sure they saw it, lol.)

It was just to deal with the anger, to fight back against the fears that the relationship coming to an end threw my way. The fear of not being enough for someone else, the fear of not finding someone who would at least love me like my ex did during the first half of things, a fear of not finding someone period.

I felt everything. Then started working on the best way to flush them out. Me writing this book alone is a testament of me doing so. Writing was one of the ways I processed a lot of the feelings I dealt with. Instead of venting to people, I started to write. I would write down how I felt about things ending, where I went wrong, where she went wrong, what we should've done differently. Everything I wanted to say, I said it to the pages of my notebook. Eventually, all of it came out. There's such power in writing your pain away.

Now, it was not the writing alone that helped all of my hurt, pain, and negativity come out. As I mentioned I also worked out and worked on other things; but, writing was a huge part. I had also dealt with the disappointment by accepting reality, constantly reminding myself that the way things were is how they were meant to will be. Every time I felt it, I would remind myself of the truth, the reality that's hard to swallow.

When I finally saw her after I grew beyond that phase, it's like I became an empty vessel. I had already felt and said everything I could've said to her in my journal. I had already cried enough, already convinced myself a life without her was enough. I had already done so much that there was nothing else to wonder, no answer to search for, or any of that. It was all out of me.

You should not run away from feelings and emotions, you must process them. You should open room to understand their purpose in this journey to mending your broken heart. Your cries will not be beautiful; you will not think the best of yourself, you will find the darkness pressing in on you from different parts. Most people will not want to hear you vent for hours, even if they love you. You will feel crazy for yelling and screaming. The anger will feel stronger than anything at times. At the end of the day, you need to do what you can to get all that negativity out of you. Whatever you must do or whatever alternatives you can come up with whether they be exercising, knitting, dancing, or writing, do them.

Understand those things are part two when it comes to dealing with the reality of the hurt; part one is looking at the pain eye-to-eye, letting it come through you and making sure it is filtered out.

Feeling used?

Feeling unworthy?

Feeling betrayed?

Feeling angry?

Feeling sad?

Feeling depressed?

Feeling pain?

Feeling lost?

Feeling lonely?

FEELING GUILTY?

REALLY MOVING ON

These are many of the feelings you will face. I wrote them here and discuss them in my "Really Moving On" course to make sure you acknowledge them and don't give them power. These feelings are common. I've felt every single one of them during the times I've been heartbroken. I worked hard to conquer them after processing them. You have to also. They keep so many people back by building insecurities that eat them in real life.

›tional chess.

One of the best things you can do is learn how to play against your emotions. Picture yourself on a chess board with your emotions. Chess is not an easy game, it requires thinking, strategy, and a level of intelligence at least for the game. You can't beat a good opponent without those things. Neither will you beat your emotions if you do not develop a way to conquer them. Learning to play against your emotion will set boundaries that you need to stick to the goal.

One thing that must be clear is, there's a difference between being aware of your emotions and battling your emotions. Being aware allows you to know what's going on and help recognize the negative plan your emotions will come with. Awareness falls into the phase we talked about earlier, how they validate the existence of a war that must be won.

Yes, I see you fighting to find healing and win yourself back as war. Yes, I called it a war; it's that important. If most people saw this as a war, they would be better prepared for it. Instead, many take it lightly and find themselves slaves to the pain and hurt for years, filled with unresolved issues, insecurities, and so much more. So yes, it's war and you have to play against it right.

How do you play emotional chess? The game of chess requires a move from both players. Let the emotions take place, you will not win by blocking them out and neglecting them. Neither will you win by allowing them to play without you playing back. You win against your emotions by making sure you're the parent and treating them as if they are the child. You win by building the right defense moves, having the right answer when they throw a fit.

For instance, when I used to get angry while dealing with my heartbreak, my first response would be to find something to do to hurt my ex back; not physically, but more taking the petty route. I felt the need to share her dark secrets with people. I felt the need to call her and give her a piece of my mind. In the younger stages of my life, I sent mean and hurtful texts as a way to cope with the anger.

During my last break-up, none of that happened. I

prepared myself for this move. Instead of writing the long text, I wrote a long letter expressing all the mean things I wanted to say to her. This killed a bunch of birds with one stone.

1.) I processed the feelings. I did not pretend these hurtful words weren't in me. Instead of being in denial and rejecting the emotions, I let myself experience them so they didn't become hidden.

2.) I responded quickly instead of letting the emotions get the best of me. I didn't entertain them for too long, letting them become overstayed feelings or push me into overthinking which would have created worse thoughts and words in my mind.

3.) I made sure they got flushed out. Writing a letter with my raw thoughts got the feelings out. This is where I knocked off one of my emotion's pieces off the board.

Having the right defense will help you reach your goal. It's important you strategize those defenses. This is why this book has a practical section to help you develop habits to you deal with all of this. The truth you must remember is that your emotions, although they feel powerful, are your child. You are the parent, you must learn to tell them no. You must learn to use the logical side of you and call them liars. It's a game you have to win to get yourself back. It's a game you have to beat to come out stronger and wiser. The more you win against it, the more it teaches you long term not to rely on your emotions when it comes to your heart and love.

Being honest with yourself.

To move on properly and find real closure, you have to be true to yourself in all the mess. You have to accept reality and reflect honestly. If you do not do this, it will be a huge roadblock in your path. You have to live through every phase of hurt to make it out of the past. By now, you should see how important it is not to bypass stages to get to the real results. There are no shortcuts to this, the road requires some real face-to-face time with the mirror.

Too often we find ourselves hiding behind pretenses and trying to make people, or ourselves, believe we are somewhere we aren't. We aspire to be those things or those stages in life we claim to be in and want the fast results. We also want the reward without the work. You can't do that; you must be honest with yourself and see yourself where you are. You can always speak things you want to see in the future; but, you should not hide behind the mask of pretense.

How do you heal when you act like you have nothing to heal from anymore even though it's right in front of your face? How do you heal from something you don't want to heal from? How can you learn from the past when you are simply running from it? You must deeply evaluate where you are and work on getting to the next place. What gets you to that next place is how much honesty is involved.

Learning to conquer your feelings and emotions is such a tough thing to win against. You can unconsciously put yourself somewhere you aren't yet. Your hunger to be on the other side of something or over something doesn't automatically take you there. It's the drive you have and the execution behind the drive that will.

Self-evaluation is the remedy. It's an important piece to the puzzle (your heart) you are trying to put together. You must ask yourself hard questions and reply to yourself honestly. *Am I over them? Do I want to be over them? What hurts me about this? Was it self-inflicted? Was I supposed to be in the relationship to begin with? Can I let them go? And so forth.* You have to get in tune with your true feelings about it all so you can know how to overcome and move forward. Confronting the hard truths and creating better solutions is a must.

A lot of people dealing with the things you are dealing with right now live in denial. They act unbothered and unmoved by the break-up. When asked about the it, they put on a poker face and deliver the best display of false happiness they can give. They act as if they already found healing, act as if they committed no wrong. They sing along all the shallow relationship quotes out there and exhibit a false sense of self-love and confidence. Ones that reek arrogance and immaturity.

The pretending can run deeper than people realize. Besides pretending to others, some start to pretend to themselves. They start to lie to themselves to create a shortcut that cannot help them. Shortcuts eat away even good things the future might bring because, eventually, you have to face yourself regardless. I've seen it countless times, people join "Team no feelings" instead of processing and conquering their emotions. Then, they say love is poison instead of acknowledging that the person or even they were the real issue.

You have to ask yourself the hard question, "Am I over them?" When you ask yourself this question and answer honestly, you will start seeing where you currently are with your healing. It lays a foundation for you to better prepare yourself for your destination or goal.

When some people start asking themselves the tough honest questions and reply honestly, they will realize how much of a difference it makes. One big question that can reroute everything is, "Do I want to be over them?" This is hard to ask which is why people don't answer it honestly. I want you to answer it honestly. After this chapter, there's a section to answer and add more questions. Now let's play devil's advocate here and say the answer is 'NO' for you. Well, this means, you will need to have a different starting ground. Instead of trying to move on, you will have to try to let go first. After that, moving on will be on your list.

The truth is, healing and closure will not come simply because part of you wants it or because it's what others say needs to happen. Part of you wanting this will not be enough, wanting it will not be enough, others saying what ought to be will not be enough. To heal and move on, all of you, has to want it, need it, see it, believe it, and work toward it, not just part of you. We do not move from where we are simply because we're not supposed to be there. It's when we don't want to be there, we do what needs to be done to move.

Sometimes people aren't moving on because they don't want to or they aren't ready to. They may not want to be over the person, they don't want to let go of hope, they don't want to find the closure. This is where being realistic will save anyone. You will know how to maneuver, you've found your real starting point. If you happen to be someone who realizes you don't want to be over your partner, it's perfectly okay. Put your focus on handling just that. Put your effort on the letting go part. However, many things said about moving on will be also crucial. You will have to control your emotions and feelings so they don't lead to making decisions you shouldn't be making, like making a fool out of yourself for someone who doesn't want you or find yourself holding on longer than you should.

In being honest with yourself, you will also learn how to be honest with those who matter in your life. What good does it do you if your friends or people think you are over someone when you don't want to be over them? What do you gain by fooling the people who can help you? What joy comes from putting energy into lying to others? Nothing good comes from pretending. It gives you more pretending to do. You will see how much more freedom you will have by not trying to live a "fake truth" or living to impress your family friends on something they just want to stand by your side for.

Yes, we will always have those friends who, in some way, will try to push us to a stage we aren't in yet. We previously spoke about how to handle that. It's best to express yourself to people who care and say or show nothing to those who don't. Fooling people shouldn't be your objective, fooling yourself most certainly should never be a thing for you.

Being honest with yourself will lead to you being honest to those who care. In some cases, they are part of this journey. Some people need their friends or support system more than they would like to admit. Putting up a façade is hard work that could be going into you being healed and truly smiling with the past behind you. You cannot move on to a new chapter if you don't finish the current chapter.

Denial is a burden. It's putting more on your back to carry during these touching times. You don't have to hold in the cry, you don't have to pretend, you don't have to convince anyone you weren't hurt or you weren't truly in love. Saying, "I'm not over them," is as important as saying, "I am ready to move on." It's okay to ask yourself the questions that force you to really look deep. If you were cheated on, ghosted, or abused, it's normal to look back to question your intention for that relationship, question the signs you missed, what was real or not, and so forth. There's nothing wrong with facing the reality of the hurt as well, and being honest with yourself about making strides to change it. Be honest with where you are, then deal with it.

Answer these questions as honestly as you can:

Am I over them?

Do I want to be over them?

What hurts me about this?

Was it self-inflicted?

Was I supposed to be in the relationship to begin with?

Can I let them go?

Write down other questions you feel are important to ask yourself below:

Misconceptions & Myths

If what we perceive to be truth is a lie, it pushes us in the wrong direction, it keeps us from getting where we want to be.

Time doesn't heal.

Everything gets better with time. When you read that saying, you agreed with it, didn't you? You're not alone, most people do. I do, too. As someone who is considered a relationship expert and a vessel of empowerment, I can tell you it took time for me to pause on that statement and include a 'but' at the end. Everything gets better with time; but, you must do your part. If everything gets better with time, what separates those who get better over time from those who gradually get worse? What could it be? Perhaps, what you personally do with the time? There's no other factor that can answer this properly.

Well, here's another popular saying for you, "Time heals all wounds." It rolls smoothly off the tongue, it makes sense, and it may have been proven right in your life before. I am sorry to break it to you, time will not heal you. I repeat, TIME WILL NOT HEAL YOU. It is a common myth that can be dangerous on this road you're traveling. A myth that has caused many to do nothing and expect something in return. You can't just expect the pain to fade, the hurt not to grow roots, or the lessons to just stick. It doesn't work that way.

Time is part of the healing process, but it can't be responsible for the healing alone. Time's job in our lives is to just be there, to exist, be present, and nothing more. What happens over time is totally up to us. What we do and how we do it. I would almost argue that there's nothing more important than understanding that time doesn't do anything but move in this process. Where will you find the desire to put in quality effort, educate yourself, discipline yourself, and heal if it's automatic? Think about it, the danger in this saying is that healing will come anyway.

It's crucial to come to a full stop and tell yourself that leaving your recovery, your healing, your growth in the hands of time won't make it happen. "Time heals all wounds," is one of the worst clichés I've heard leave people's lips when speaking to those dealing with heartbreak. It's not always harmful advice being spewed; but, it does give people the idea that as time goes by, all will dissolve on its own and things will simply get better. This is not true. Nothing truly dissolves this way, it simply gets pushed aside without being dealt with.

Time will help you put the experience in the back of your mind, it doesn't mean you are healed. Over time, you won't be as hung up on your ex, you may forget them, you may not cry anymore, you may not grow angry anymore, you may even be in a new relationship. None of that means you got better or healed.

Moving with time doesn't mean moving forward. Unless you are proactively confronting the issues to heal, time is prolonging the process. Even more dangerous, it's helping you hide them deeper with the mindset that everything is gone. You have to do your part. And yes, your part will take time, but it doesn't depend on time. Again, it's what you do over time.

The misconception is that, if time is involved in both the good or the bad, it must be controlling the ship. You are controlling the ship, time is the ocean. You either get to your destination or sink. The ocean doesn't determine the outcome. How well equipped your ship is, how good of a captain you are, and how you navigate through the big waves decides for you. This popular saying sometimes keeps people dwelling far too long and helps depression swallow too many people while waiting for a life jacket from time. We have to stop thinking that existing as the clock keeps ticking will pull us out of the heartbreak.

I've met a fair amount of people who did nothing but let time work its magic. Out of their mouths I've heard them say they were no longer attached to things of the past while the bad of the past puppeted them around. I've heard people claim they're better because they survived their last heartbreak failing to realize that some of their fears and insecurities came from that heartbreak. I've been in relationships with women who were convinced they'd gotten over their ex only to see emotions flare when asked about them or to talk about the experience. These are the types of results letting time heal you will lead to.

When you leave your healing, closure, and preparation for the next relationship in the hands of time, it is considered 'out of sight, out of mind' healing. That is another way of saying, "Brush the mess under the carpet. As long you don't trip over it it's fine." It's not fine; it will not be fine.

As a father of a young boy, one of the things my son

has trouble staying consistent with is cleaning his room. It's something we demand of him every day before bedtime. On many nights, he gets it done but even when he does, he rushes through it, meaning it's most likely not done right. Part of my routine is to check the room when he claims it's done. Most of the time, the room looks amazing! I head right to the bed and take a look under it. Why? Because under the bed is always a mess.

Instead of doing the hard work, oftentimes he chooses a shortcut that makes the room appear clean. It appears finished because all the mess has been shifted to where it can't be seen. This is the same thing as letting time be your captain. It moves the mess somewhere it will not disrupt the illusion of healing most develop. It hides the chaos and shows you what can be seen and accepted. The true test will come when you see that ex or hear something about them, or find yourself in a new relationship still hanging on to habits and behaviors birthed from that relationship. When things aren't dealt with, they eventually find their way to the surface. Deal with them.

Over time, things can get better, you can be happier,

you can be whole, confident, and trusting again. Over time, you will start believing in love again, open to dating again. Over time, you will not remember the things hurting you right now. Many things can get better with time. It is your job to make sure that happens.

Out of sight, out of mind.

What you don't see can kill you faster than something you do. Years ago, I worked for a propane company and one of the most lifesaving things I learned is that propane is odorless. They had to give it an odor. If a truck of propane was somehow delivered to us odorless, we were to return it right away. This was a mistake that rarely happened; but, it did. I experienced it and it was a big deal.

Why was the odor so important? Because you can have a gas leak right in front of you and not smell it. Imagine being 20 feet away from a grill, sparking a match away from the gas tank and a fire comes alive. An incident like that can alter anyone's life. Along with propane, there are many other things in this world that you can't see but can do serious harm to you. Heartbreak may not kill you, it may never lead to any physical damage (though it happens), but it can definitely do harm without notice.

Unlike physical pain, emotional pain is something we process differently. We don't run to help when we are faced with heartache, we run the opposite way. We run away from what hurt us. The sweet joy we once felt when we were in our partner's presence becomes an annoying series of events that reminds us of something bad. Who wants to be in the presence of the person who hurt them, or even deeper, next to anything that reminds them of who hurt them. No one that is.

Instead, we want to be where pain doesn't control the air, where we are less disturbed about the situation, where we tune out the harsh reality, where we have peace by no longer sharing our space with them. This is what gives the term 'out of sight, out of mind' so much meaning to many learning to put a relationship that didn't work behind them. It became another good saying, with great intentions that can be misinterpreted. Unfortunately, the misinterpretations tend to give birth to misconceptions that keep people from doing the deep internal work that needs to be done.

After a break-up, some relocate to a different city, state, or even country. It's the idea of running away from what is holding you back. This can be a healthy thing to do if it needs to be done. The goal is to move on in a way that works best for you. If disconnecting from everything you currently know so nothing can spark the memories is the way for you, so be it. Some people need to change their environment to hit the restart button and wave goodbye to the past. This is something I may even recommend to certain people who are in the position for that.

Now that we are clear there is nothing wrong with getting away from memories to establish new ones, let's talk about the 'out of sight, out of mind' mindset. One that can keep people from clinging to healing and move on.

When someone starts to rely on this idea as a way to escape their reality too much, it can become problematic. Just as we spoke about time not being able to do the work itself, it stands for this saying as well. Making sure your ex is as far away from you as possible may be a good thing. It can also become something that causes you to grow dormant and lose focus on your healing.

One of the things I learned in life is understanding healing doesn't come without confrontations and growth. At times it doesn't come without discomfort. You not being confronted by their presence or experiencing some discomfort because of them makes it easy to take your feet off the gas and not prioritize your goal. See, one of the things that will motivate you to stay on your journey to move on and continue to put in work is self-test. When your ex is mentioned or you come across them face-to-face, your emotions will rise up. Thoughts will fill your head; your heart may skip beats. An internal or external reaction will come from you. As it's happening, you will not see anything good in it; but, it will be a great measure to show how much progress you have made.

I remember this clearly with my last failed relationship. My ex and I attended the same church. This means I saw her every Wednesday or Sunday. This became challenging for both of us. It started out with us pretending not to see each other to her slowly disappearing. In a matter of months, she stopped going to our church.

Things went from being extremely hard for me, which motivated me to write a lot, pray a lot, and live in the gym, to being smooth. I went months not seeing her and telling myself I needed to overcome the break-up. Then, one day she showed up at our church and I did not know how to act. A wave of emotions hit me, the pretending started to come back, questions started to rob my peace of mind, the urge to approach her was there. I felt ways I hadn't felt before.

I left church thinking about her, wanting to text her, wondering what I could text her. Then I searched her social media to find out who was the "new person" in her life and what she'd been up to. I spent a week thinking about her. Luckily for me, the next week she didn't come. Everything I experienced slowly faded away. Until...you guessed it, she came back again. Everything I hadn't felt in the months before came back. Every time I saw her, it sparked something.

"I miss you" texts were sent, meet ups were arranged, and harsh truths were shared every time she came back. All the times she re-appeared, I forced myself to stay committed to my internal work. I was in the best shape of my life, my career was going good, I was in a better place in life. I soon realized that every time she came around, it was easier for me to handle everything. I started caring less about her showing up, my heart wouldn't beat anymore, not an ounce of pretense would show up, I would genuinely greet her on a platonic level. The urge to start a conversation died out, the anger couldn't find a spark, the bitterness became quieter. I simply became less and less interested in going back.

The discomfort that came from seeing her in the early days made me realize internally I needed to do some work. All throughout those times when someone asked me if I was over her, I swore by it. Yet, seeing her made me feel the opposite of that. Through self-reflection, I realized not seeing her in some way caused me to get lazy. I would skip work outs, buy relationship books that I wouldn't finish, and I even wrote less.

That's the subtle trap in 'out of sight, out of mind.' It makes us ease off and sometimes helps us believe we are somewhere we haven't yet arrived. One important thing I mentioned to a client of mine which I think bears repeating is, "Younow you're over someone when they are in your sight and they don't occupy your mind." I broke down how not seeing them does nothing but help us hide behind our own lies. The right measuring stick is when their presence doesn't move us at all.

In my personal opinion, I believe that ex was experiencing the same things I am speaking about right now. She would show up for a few services, then disappear for long periods of time. In moments when I worked my way to speaking to her, it led to her being gone for longer periods of time. I believe each time she thought she was over it all and had made tremendous progress, she would suck it up and put herself in the same environment as me to realize there was still healing and moving on that needed to be done. It pushed her to go back to her ways. Granted, it's a hard thing to do, it's also a measuring stick that can be needed for some.

'Out of sight, out of mind' is a great practice, it's a healthy way to cope with things even if only a certain period of time. To win this battle, we must identify all weaknesses and there is one in that mindset. It's a belief that can get you stuck and hurt our progress and internal work. I've had countless coaching sessions with clients who rebooked my service simply because they came face-to-face with an ex-partner and realized that the work wasn't done as they truly thought. Cherish this concept but don't rely on it for your healing.

Over-busyness is a thing.

Find yourself working more? Spending more time at the gym, even getting yourself lost in a new hobby. Escapism is one of our go-tos when it comes to dealing with heartbreak. There's no better way to get your mind off your current reality than to get lost in new things and create new memories. Being busy helps us achieve that. It keeps our bodies moving and our minds jumping between different things which ultimately keeps our heart at peace, in a sense numb to the torment. This is a coping method that helps many move on faster than they realize. It can also be another subtle distraction that has kept some from healing.

You may say, "Oh no, Pierre. Staying busy is helpful. How can it ever be a bad thing?" I agree one hundred percent with you. Being busy is a very healthy way to cope with it all once done with the right intentions. However, like everything else, balance is always needed or it will be another way to run instead of confronting what is in front of you. Without balance, you can easily find yourself off the deep ends or not swimming at all. Both are dangerous when you are trying to stay afloat.

One of the things I had to learn in life, like many children, is how to properly communicate, as well as be on the receiving end of communication respectfully. Just like other kids, when I listened to someone talk, I wanted them to get to the point or I'd zone out.

I disliked eye contact. It was the thing I got in trouble for when I was younger. To the teachers it was rude; but, to me, it was trying to find the best way to actively listen. I couldn't stop my eyes from wondering off or keep myself from being anxious to get my words in. I needed to get better at listening and not making my lack of interest so noticeable. I started by making my eyes focus as much as possible on whoever was speaking. As someone with bad hearing, sometimes I focused too much on the person's lips to make out the words. Over time, I noticed this way was making people uncomfortable. I was paying attention to what they were saying, but my eye contact was too aggressive.

Believe it or not, there were times I stared so deeply that the person would shrink right in front of my eyes. They would get smaller and smaller and the sound of their voice would fade. This wasn't the right way. I tried to compensate for that by not making any eye contact at all as a quick fix to my issue. I would stare down at the ground or have my eyes wandering everywhere like I used to do when running.

As a cross country and track starter, looking down helped me stay at the right pace in 5k runs. Instead of looking at my destination, looking down shortened the distance in my mind, it made the distance more bearable. I did this while people talked to me and occasionally looked up as a sign that I was listening. Of course, that didn't work.

I had to change this approach. People considered it to be a rude gesture and thought I was uninterested in what they had to say. Over time, I worked on it and found the perfect balance. I would make eye contact, then over focus on something near their face, then zoom out again focus on them and keep repeating a cycle like this. Looking away was something I occasionally did as well, only for a short period of time. Instead of doing one or the other, I learned to find a balance and do all the things that did not work before in a different way. I learned to keep the appropriate focus while engaging more. This sharpened my communication skills.

You must have the same mindset towards a broken heart. We ought to not focus too much on the pain or too much on things outside of it. You must learn to keep your eyes on what is important and keep yourself engaged in this battle to win yourself back.

When you reach too far into busyness, it's easy to find yourself disengaged, losing focus without cause, running away from your heartbreak instead of slowly escaping as you outgrow the old things. The problem is when many start using overbusyness to cope with the hard part. This is when people double down on what they are doing, picking up more things than they can handle, finding themselves too busy to work on their healing.

Excessive busyness can be almost as unproductive as over-dwelling. It can subtly breed complacency and eat away the consistency that is needed to bring the pieces back together. There's power in acknowledging the past or being aware of the current struggle to use it as a compass leading you to better. Even when you're not pretending, overbusyness can subconsciously lead you to believe everything is okay when nothing is.

This is why being busy must be monitored. This is why it's important to question yourself from time-to-time. Checking in with yourself by asking questions like, "Why am I doing these things?" or simply slowing down can make you more aware. Being busy will leave you unaware of your emotional state quickly. As the popular quote discusses, you have to know the past to build a better future or to not let history repeat itself. The past itself is not harmful but how you use it can be harmful and counterproductive to your goal. Keeping yourself busy to run away from the past is not the way to go. Staying busy while walking away from your past is the path that breeds healing.

Relationships end because of failure.

In life, nothing stays the same. We have different seasons, nights and days, hot and cold. Things change. More importantly, some things work out and some things just don't. The same thing goes for relationships; some relationships will work, some won't.

Out of the ones that do not work out, not all of them end because they are a failure. This is a truth that some people need to reconcile with to take bigger steps into their journey forward. There are countless people who will continuously struggle to find their way to move on simply because they are consumed by self-assigned guilt, shame, and misunderstanding.

It's common that people find it easy to blame their exes, but there's a group of people who solely focus on blaming themselves. Those people have to renew their mindset before they can get to the letting go part. When you believe something is your fault, grieving it doesn't become a phase, it becomes a chain that keeps you living in regret until you force yourself out of that. Self-assigned guilt and shame may be what's eating everything away but there's always a bigger picture. The root of the self-assigned guilt is formed by the idea that this heartbreak is all your fault because the relationship did not just end.

Imagine this, if you saw a relationship as just another phase in life, wouldn't it be easier to transition out of that phase? Or you started looking at things ending as part of your journey to love instead of proof that you failed to keep the love you had alive. The idea that a relationship not working out is a flat-out failure that you contributed to, keeps far more than enough people dwelling in regret. What did I do? What didn't I do? What should I have done differently? Will I find someone like this again? Am I worthy of love? Will anyone ever love me again? This mindset keeps you stuck in cycle of soul sucking questions that point to you as the problem. It keeps you living in "why" mode instead of the doing mode.

This is where important lessons are missed. Benefits from the experience aren't tapped into. Closing the chapter becomes the last focus instead of re-reading it or re-living it all. It's crucial if you're at the stage to tell yourself these things. Maybe neither of you were the best fit for each other even though you're both great people. Maybe this was a foundation piece you both needed to learn how to be great lovers later on. Maybe being together opened both of your eyes to some preferences you weren't open to. Maybe the relationship is the beginning step of a great platonic friendship.

Relationships happen for different reasons and they also end for different reasons. Their ending doesn't always reflect anything but another part of your journey. This is something I always speak against along with the popular thought about soul mates.

I've run into a fair share of people who believe God only picked one person for them since the beginning of time and that's the one they will marry. Even as a man of faith, I question this. What if I got married at a time I wasn't walking with God? How could it be destined if I'm out of God's will? What if my future wife decides to stay in an unhealthy relationship and never bump into me? What if my soul mate no longer wants to be my soul mate and divorces me?

We all have free will. Many of us do what we want instead of what God wants many times. Someone missed it somewhere in this human life and went outside what was meant to be. Now, I strongly believe if two people are walking with God, He can pair them into a beautiful union. That doesn't mean they were soul mates since the beginning. That ideology keeps some fighting for lifeless relationships and terrible marriages that shouldn't have even existed to start with.

It's crucial to keep in mind that a relationship doesn't define you, it doesn't define whether you are worthy of love or not. A relationship coming to an end isn't always a failure. It isn't always a missed opportunity; they may not have gotten away. Maybe they were making room for who is for you. The truth is you will meet other people, find someone else to love, a new relationship to apply your lessons to. You will move on. You don't have to live in regret, relationships are not as black and white as success or failure. There's more to the experience than a shot at destiny.

What doesn't kill you doesn't make you stronger.

What doesn't kill you sometimes keeps you living in fear and controlled by past experiences. How many times have you heard this? Not often. That is why I am saying it. We must kill the misconception to get to the core of certain things. This is one of those sayings we must properly address to chase healing with the right shoes on.

Why is speaking about this important? Because what didn't kill you may have given you tons of insecurities, created some irrational fears, and helped you develop some dysfunctional habits you aren't aware of. It may have also given you a false idea of strength or caused you to live in false reality. No, whatever doesn't kill you doesn't make you stronger. It can also form weaknesses you don't even realize are weighing you down.

As a relationship coach, I've had clients who would boldly say, "I am stronger because of that relationship." They meant it and seemingly lived by it. This is the truth for many people. Once they overcome a bad relationship, they simply grow and learn not to fall into the same traps again.

The other side of that is some don't grow stronger. The thing with some of my clients is that when I got under the hood, I saw they were living under a façade. Surviving something doesn't automatically make you strong. Sometimes it only sharpens your survival skills. This is where the problem lies; relationships aren't meant to be survived. They are meant to be lived and enjoyed.

Out of those clients, once we started to dig deeper into their past relationships to better understand what their current reality was, I would often detect behaviors that stemmed from those past relationships. We would identify defense mechanisms put in place with good intention but harming their new relationship. We would see trust issues that are justifiable but that only form guilt trips for their current partner. We would see boundaries that made sense, but, at the root were walls placed to keep people similar to those who've hurt them out. They may have overcome past relationships that made them stronger in some sense but still killing areas of their lives.

Where this mindset does the most damage is not

the insecurities, the fears, the bad habits. It's the false sense of strength and confidence.

Them moving on is a beautiful sign.

When you are in the process of moving on and progressing beautifully, nothing will come to test and attack your growth more than finding out your ex is moving on. It's something you have to prepare yourself for because it's bound to happen. You will either hear about it, see it on social media, or simply run into them with their new partner.

When that day comes, you will most likely get a tug at your heart. You will probably feel hurt, maybe shocked, even disappointed. Negative emotions will try to rise up, tears may even find their way to your eyes afterwards. You will probably pretend, you will probably say some untrue things if you get to exchange words. You may act awkward. As long you don't react, you are in good hands. As long as you don't let your current emotions take over, you'll be alright.

How you feel in the moment really doesn't matter. Neither does it define anything in your journey. How you process it afterwards will make the most difference. Keep this in mind because it will be the last thing on your mind.

Plenty of questions will flood your thoughts after different emotions hit you. When it happens, you have to pay attention to yourself; this is where self-awareness will have to be prioritized.

This is where most of the things discussed in previous sections of this book will come handy. You will have to redirect everything to see the good in the event. You will have to choose to find the good in it all. This is a sign, a sign that you are not supposed to be together. Is it truly? Well, it doesn't matter. You have to use it as fuel to move on instead of it being the reason to run back and wallow in the heartbreak. Them moving on will present you with an opportunity to stare at the reality right in the face and say, "I have to accept it. This is my sign to move forward with my life."

Too often, people let seeing their ex moving on to someone else pull the worst out of them. They take ten steps back after three forward. Their first reaction is to bash their ex, then they research the ex's new partner trying to find wrongs that will validate their sense of jealousy. They subconsciously develop negative feelings against a person who they most likely know nothing about. They become offended at the fact their ex is putting the relationship behind them too fast. They also start a dialogue in their mind of whether their ex is moving on to better or not. Whether they are happy or faking it. Whether the new partner knows what the ex did to them? What has the ex said about them to the new person...

Let me be the first to tell you it is easy to put your focus on everything you cannot control at that time, everything that will knock you off your goal. Part of getting to a place where you "Really Move On" is taking everything that comes at you to use as stepping stones. Them moving on is a sign that you should move on as well. It's a reminder to let go of what already let you go. Take it as your ex is making it clear that nothing will happen between you both. Yes, they may have moved on too fast. Yes, your ex may spew some lies about you. Yes, they may be a better partner to your ex. So what? Your ex is none of your concern anymore. They have someone else to worry about them.

It may even be a yes to your golden question, "Is

he/she really moving on or this is just a thing?" IT DOES NOT MATTER! Your focus is on you really moving on.

When you are aware that they've started entertaining someone else, this has to become what helps you speed up rather than something that slows you down. You can't let the situation abuse you, you must use it. They are telling you to go, telling you to stop wondering about the two of you, telling you that he/she doesn't care about you anymore. It's your key to, not only close the door, but lock it shut. It's your sign to leave it all behind. Enough people don't see it that way but you have to. In order to really move on, you have to use everything at your disposal. Make the best of what pulls out the worst out of many.

Healing

Healing is the root for growth, it's what takes us into a better version of ourselves, helps us taste more maturity, and introduces us to a better future.

Healing is a priority.

To fully move on, you have to put healing first. You have to keep it at the top of your priority list, letting no one cause you to get off that journey. No one truly moves on until they are healed enough. How can your heart be in good shape when it is still damaged goods? How can happiness live in there when pain is taking up most of the space? How can you ever meet any form of love without healing? Healing is the answer to many things.

What is healing? Healing is being on the other side of what hurt you. It's the growth and maturity you have reached after enduring and overcoming the pain. It's being at peace with all that has happened and no longer living as a victim to it. Healing is not about making your heart completely whole, but rather cleaning up the pieces as you put them back together more carefully. It's focusing on dealing with things internally before you try to move on externally.

The unfortunate thing is that healing isn't prioritized enough. Far too many try to run circles around healing instead of diving into it. Many say they are trying to heal when they are simply trying to get away from the pain and put the experience behind them. The interesting part about healing is you can let go and move on without healing. You can no longer desire your ex, no longer have to deal with the emotional battles but still aren't healed. You can put the situation in the past but never heal. This is why healing must be prioritized because without it you can move steps forward and miss quite a bit.

Healing requires moving on beyond the surface. It's the deep, internal work that needs to be done, not only to be in a better space, but be better overall. Healing is what prepares people for a next relationship with the right outlook, understanding, focus, and so forth. Until you are healed, you can easily become who hurt you. The experience may shape you in ways that aren't toxic but can do subtle damage in the future.

For instance, there are countless people who are in relationships right now that will not thrive simply because they learned from their last relationship anything close to being dependent on your partner is a weakness. To be clear, they don't see it as weakness but "a weakness." The idea hasn't been fully vilified in their eyes although they still think it's unsafe. The reality is that no relationship can survive without interdependency; codependency is what they are afraid of. However, the unhealed part of them causes everything to blend together because it is better to be safe than sorry. Their belief is that it puts you in a situation to get hurt, it leaves you too vulnerable. It creates subtle beliefs from the unhealed parts of your life and shapes your future outlook.

There's nothing wrong with a woman being independent and codependency has been used against too many women far too long for them not to set guidelines in their lives. It's justifiable, but it will not keep a healthy relationship with a man who needs emotional attachment and wants to pour his soul into the relationship instead of just enough. It can go both ways, of course. This a common theme I see out in the dating world.

Without healing, you do not get all the good that ought to come from the experience. You only learn how to survive the next one. This only helps protect you from what you can see; not your blindside. The next relationship may bring issues you have never dealt with before. You may fall into a different hole while trying to make sure you don't fall into the same one. It's crucial to set yourself on a path to see a better you, a version of you that has grown and matured out of the experience. You can't settle for being just okay. You can't just let go. You can't just put it behind. You don't want to waste your experience and pain. Being better is right in the hands of healing. Put your focus towards that, this is what will help you REALLY move on.

Closure comes in doses.

As you are reflecting, unlearning and relearning, and healing, it's important to understand closure is something that comes in parts. It's not something you wake up one day and say, "Boom! It's here." It manifests itself into raw evidence long after it started happening.

Like everything with moving on, there's no siren, no notification, nothing that makes you aware you have moved into a different phase. It's all in the state of awareness. Unless you understand how closure will come, you will not know what closure is or feels like when it has arrived.

Closure, by definition, is when all the pieces of a relationship are hung up; when the chapter is finally closed. It's when the pain is gone, the memories are just meaningless events, and your ex is just someone you've known. There's a sense of finality with closure. There's nothing left, no residue or anything of that nature. That, my friend, will not happen in one day, neither is it something that will take forever. It's in between; yet, that's not how many of us see it.

We wait for the day closure will come. We wait and wait feeling like we are far behind without realizing every bit of what we are doing takes steps to closure. We wait for a big moment that seems to be far away or a miracle to fall upon us one day.

When it comes to closure, we must see it in increments, we must see it in process, we must have the mindset that we are finding it as we are working hard to move forward. Like many other things in life, the destination is only a part of it. The process is often the most important part.

It's like looking at the current state of someone who's become successful. They are congratulated and celebrated for where they are. Some even envy their position without realizing all the steps taken on that journey. What is often missed are the years of hard work, consistency, failure, and perseverance. The success is just the stamp for others to see, a visual proof of it all. It's really the process being magnified.

Closure comes the same way. It's a process of you healing and growing. It's getting small wins piece-by-piece.

It's reaching your goals in different parts of moving on before you've fully moved on. Closure will come in visual proof for you or some type of emotional evidence. The truth will be that it's been happening. It's simply coming to you in doses.

Maybe you learn to forgive them first while still working on learning to forgive yourself. Doesn't mean you haven't taken a step forward. Maybe you learned to let go of the impulse decisions, the emotionally driven decisions. It doesn't mean all the feelings are gone. Maybe you have it settled in the reality that you can't be with the person but you haven't fully processed the reality the two of you will never be. Nothing happens all at once on this journey, it takes place in parts over time.

What you must understand as you're moving on is if you're lacking in one area, try to look into the area you aren't lacking. People give up so easily when the parts they haven't grown out of are tested or put on display. I've seen people return to relationships after forgiving their partner, simply because they couldn't forgive themselves. They use forgiving their partner as a reason to give that chapter a try once again when it's clear there is more denial, more of not wanting to accept the fact you picked them and they didn't pick you.

I've seen people who've accepted that their partners have moved on, but can't forgive them and dang sure can't forget. I've seen people live miserably for months because they couldn't find the closure they were looking for. Closure is a process of progress; it's never proof that nothing is happening.

One day, it'll fully manifest itself in your life. You'll be living your life, not concerned about them one bit. Seeing them with someone else won't bother you one bit, you won't hold anything against yourself for that relationship or any other. Your heart will have no bitterness hidden in it, no anger towards them. You'll be a better version of you waiting for love to come.

One day you'll get your closure. Understand it will be little things adding up to the big picture. Do not give up if it's not coming all at once. Use the small steps to keep going.

Seek growth, not revenge.

One of the most powerful voices we have is our silence. Doing nothing in many cases takes more strength and courage than doing something. One of the biggest parts of anyone's healing is draining themselves of the desire to react and prove themselves to the wrong people.

When things end, what keeps people from moving on is the cycle they put themselves into. A cycle that repels growth but seeks revenge. People usually start to operate by emotions more than they should, letting their feelings guide them into cycles motivated by hurt.

After break-ups, it's easy to act on impulse. It's common to see people making decisions in an attempt to convince their ex that life is better without them, that they've moved on, or are happily single. This leads to them going places they can't afford, hanging out with friends they shouldn't be with and who aren't even real friends, going out on dates with people they know they have no business with hoping to run into their exes to pretend and show off. Many find themselves in beds they shouldn't be in, giving themselves away to people they shouldn't as a way to cope with the break-up or get revenge.

To heal, you cannot seek revenge. You cannot let your emotions convince you to act petty or stoop too low. As human beings, it is in our nature to push back when someone pushes us down. When a failed relationship is what pushes you down, you must focus on getting up instead of pushing back.

You cannot move on properly or heal if you allow yourself to fall into the madness of chasing revenge. It's hard to find self-love and peace when you are doing so. You are only inviting more pain in and allowing regret to score more points on you. Do not pursue revenge trying to break their heart or give them a taste of their own medicine. This is not a good investment of your time or energy. It can be tempting but you must learn to stay on a different path. You must remind yourself that you are chasing healing which requires you to take the high road on many things.

They've let you go, you don't need their attention. I understand fighting back is a common way to react; you don't have to take the common route. You are reading this because you know the common routes don't lead to the right destinations. A better version of you is what you should be fighting for. You only need to fight to impress the old you.

Everything should be about who you are in the mirror and improving that person. When you start trying to show your ex that you have upgraded, you are downgrading. You are putting your focus on less productive things which is going backwards and letting immaturity get the best of you. When you start hanging out with friends who you are only involved with because of this phase you are in, you build superficial and toxic relationships. Some of those relationships may become good friendships, though in most cases, it's searching for companionship anywhere you can find it.

Going out on dates with people you shouldn't be with welcomes more bad choices causing more damage. Seeking revenge is also where morality seems to blur for many. The no-no's become things you are okay with because it's payback. I can't even count how often I've heard stories of people who get their hearts broken and start entertaining their ex's friends or family members, or people who've simply given them attention before. No one should let hurt pull them that low.

People make lots of choices in the revenge phase without realizing it does nothing to their ex. However, it puts them a further distance away from their healing. As a matter of fact, it gives your ex ammunition to say you were a poor partner or human being. Most people end up embarrassing themselves. The unfortunate thing is that those who are using it as a coping mechanism can't see how clouded their vision is by their pretense. They don't see how the end of the relationship makes them feel so rejected, so unworthy, and incapable of being loved, so they must do something to make them feel good somehow. This is how some people end up in a cycle of toxic relationships. They start chasing revenge, to later realize nothing good came from it.

To happily move on and find real closure, you have to live for you after relationships end. Focus on growth more than revenge. Make new friends as you grow, rather than build weak relationships to occupy yourself. Date when you are ready, not to show them you've moved on. Ignore their calls and texts because you are trying to move on, not because you want them to see how it felt when they were doing it to you. Become better for you, not to be better than them. When you do things for yourself, you heal, you grow, you let go in peace.

When you don't seek revenge, you see clearer. With clearer vision, you get to your destination with less hassle. Growth > Revenge.

Forgive them.

Forgiveness is the river you will have to drink from to find healing. You cannot heal until you forgive them; you absolutely cannot. You may have heard this before, maybe too many times before but it bears repeating. You cannot heal until you forgive them. You can most certainly move on; but, healing will not come until you take this difficult step. The freedom or peace you are looking for requires you to do this.

This is easy to say and, of course, harder to do; it must be done. I know how you feel. It sucks when the person who made you believe they could hold your heart in their hands and protect it became the one who smashed it into pieces. It ought to be a crime, right? And in some cases, what caused the relationship to end is unforgivable.

Here's the thing, forgiving them is an act of love towards yourself not them. Forgiving them is for you. It's pulling yourself from under the weight of the situation to save your heart from getting clogged up by hate, anger, jealousy, and anything else that comes with being in your position. It's making sure what happened to you has no control over you, your thoughts, emotions, feelings, and mind.

When you don't forgive, you hold the situation in, sometimes storing it deep into your heart where only certain triggers remind you that those feelings are there. It's planting poison in a garden you want to grow love. When the situation exists in your thoughts, your memories, and is stored in your soul, it slowly gains a power that can even destroy you.

Not forgiving affects you in ways you will not realize. It can turn you into someone you never expected. When you don't forgive, you walk around carrying resentment, a level of hate and hurt inside of you. Those emotions are heavy on the soul. They are not meant to reside in your life. To preserve the good in you, fight for the good in you, the faith left in love, the strength left to love and so on, you must forgive.

I didn't realize how heavy unforgiveness was until I struggled to forgive an ex in my past. When the heartbreak happened, it was tough on me. I couldn't eat, I felt betrayed, I felt fooled. For months I lived with an anger boiling in me, I kept imagining the worst of her. How could she say she loved me when she wasn't there for me while I was suffering and even worse, was the reason I was suffering?

I gradually went from being hurt to being hungry for revenge, my thoughts went to a dark place about her. I also began to become molded by it. I started developing this mean spirit when interacting with women. I started believing love was a tool people used to get what they needed. I found myself even saying things like, "Love hurts."

I acted as if I happily lived the single life when I really grew miserable. This experience was one of the things that led me into my womanizer phase. My thirst for love seemed to dry up, left unquenched. All I wanted was just one thing from women. Ever hear people talk about certain types of people they don't date such as people from a certain race, certain careers, or body characteristics? That was me. I started to build a resentment, not only towards her, but people who matched her physical description. I found myself changing my dating preferences, building negative feelings towards people I didn't know solely because they belonged to a group of people.

It became easier to justify certain stereotypes and make questionable generalizations because of the bad experience. This was where I did a full stop. One of the things I detested growing up was people judging me by the color of my skin, my heritage, or my community. I always went above and beyond to not do the same.

As a thinker, once I began to evaluate what I was doing, the hypocrisy started bothering me. I was able to look in the mirror, deep into my life, and question what was happening. It took a while; I eventually put a finger on it.

The answer is, I never forgave the person who hurt me the most. Instead of doing so, I started treating far too many people as the enemy. I started looking at people as possible threats who might hurt me like my ex. I didn't see myself being the one doing the hurting as it was happening.

As I continued to deeply reflect, I chose to forgive her. It needed to be done. It didn't happen in an instant; but I chose to forgive her. Every bad thought that came, I spoke against. I spoke affirmations on forgiveness. I prayed. I wrote. I even watched how I spoke about her to other people. I forced myself to forgive them. Man! A weight lifted off my shoulder when that negativity lightened. It felt freeing, like the tension that releases when you apologize about something. It got off my chest and I felt my heart beating again. I never told them anything about this or even had a conversation with them after the relationship ended. I did, however, write them letters as part of my writing exercise that were never sent.

Before I started writing poems for women, I was a blogger who wrote about relationships. My focus was on highlighting the men, defending them, and standing up for them. I felt it was necessary to give them credit in a society that seems to feel the need to speak ill of them.

I spoke on the battles they also face because of terrible men, their insecurities, the things they desire, and their experiences with bad women as well. Often, this would upset some of the women who read my relationship content. Privately, many men would thank me for speaking for them. Many women would also thank me because it helped them reflect and understand. However, there were those who felt like men are scum who only know how to hurt women, so whatever I said was invalid.

In the early years, I argued with those women. I quickly learned that no matter what I said, even if it was true, they would not receive it. I changed how I approached my comment section over time, from responding to observing and even having private conversations with those people. One thing I discovered is that many of them were simply hurt. The hurt made it hard for them to accept that good men exist or any good can come from men. I later concluded I can't help those women see men better, I can only help them focus on healing; most importantly, forgiving which will lead to them accepting the truth.

When you don't forgive people, it becomes hard to see outside the hurt, outside the pain. Until those women do the internal things to forgive the men for themselves, they will always carry bitterness they can't see eating the up their joy, their ability to comprehend some realities, and so forth.

The ultimate act of forgiveness is also forgetting. Yes, I'm saying what you think you've read. FORGIVE AND

FORGET. Until I started applying this, it was hard keeping forgiveness active. Forgiveness is not just saying I am freeing you of this sin; it's also making sure it stays that way.

Many think it's garbage advice to tell someone to forget, but it's wise counsel. Counsel so difficult to execute people will suggest you do the opposite and lean into what you would naturally do. This entire book is about choosing what is right instead of going with what feels right, yet is wrong.

Forgive and forget is not about acting like whatever happened never happened. It's not being naïve. It's about finding freedom and burying the situation in the past. It's about caring for your heart and your soul and doing whatever it takes to heal and nurture them properly.

How can something be in the past when you keep it present? Forgetting is about the experience, not getting a chance to bring itself and the pain into your future. It's about detaching yourself from the experience so it can no longer have power over you.

You may ask, 'What about the lessons I learned? Should I forget them?' No, I do not want you to. The truth about this is, no one forgets the lessons learned through hurt. If there's something we are good at as humans, it is remembering what hurt us and how we got hurt. I know not to touch a hot stove because I've gotten burned. I don't remember when it happened, where I was, or who left the stove on. I just remember not touch a stove when it's on because it burns.

To keep in context with what I just said, let's use the stove as if it is the person from your past. I forgave the stove, I put the stove in the past. Years later, the lesson still resonates inside of me. The difference is, I don't remember which stove it was, the color, the model, or whether it was gas or electric. If I saw the stove, I wouldn't have any negative emotions towards it. It's a done deal. It taught me what I needed. I carried the lessons and left the experience behind. I know it's not that simple. With a stove, there are no emotions, no attachments just memories but it's still relevant. This is the approach we must have to truly forgive and move beyond the experience.

As I began writing this, an old friend shared a Facebook memory photo with me in a group chat. It was me thanking him for making me laugh that day and how it helped me get my mind off things. He asked me, "What were you going through?" One of my other close buddies replied, "Probably got his heartbroken again," in short answer. My reply was, "It's probably true!"

Nothing hurt me more than heartbreaks in my younger years. I should have been able to remember who it was and what happened in that relationship quickly, yet I didn't. To be honest, I remember a lot of my exes by their lessons and nothing more. In many cases, when I speak about them, I speak about what I did wrong to mess up the relationship. This is just the end result of me forgiving and forgetting. Some of those experiences taught me so much. They contributed to the great husband my wife knows, the insightful author I've become and poet who's become a mouthpiece to so many.

When you're in pain, it doesn't feel like there are lessons in it but there are. You have to treat it like fruit. You eat the part that's edible and leave the seed or the core behind. This is what I did. For you, the seed or inedible part may be hurt, pain, betrayal, or disappointment. The goal is to leave the experience in the past and keep the lesson. It's the lessons that will save you. Choosing to constantly remember the experience will only keep replaying a hurtful part of your life.

Forgive them and forget it all. This is how you keep fears and insecurities away. Then, rise above it all and heal. You don't need to be holding on to the memories to remember the lessons. You don't need to resurrect what is meant to be dead and buried. Let it all go. If you have to, ask yourself, 'Why am I holding on to this experience, besides the fact it did some damage?'

None of us escape life without pain. This is where I say live and learn. You deserve to be free, controlled by nothing. Forgive, forgive, forgive, and forget. This is even biblical if you are a fellow believer. God says to forgive those who trespass us because he knows the type of hinderance it will cause in our lives. Again, forgive, forgive, forgive, and forget.

Forgive yourself.

Once you are done being honest with yourself and your focus is right, it's time to begin focusing on a different type of forgiveness. It's time to work on forgiving yourself. Yes, you need forgiveness from yourself.

Many people are overdue for their own self-forgiveness. It's right behind forgiving others as one of the hardest things we must do. The unfortunate thing is, not many people believe that is something they must do. Lack of self-forgiveness is one of the things that keeps us as far away from healing as can be. It's hard to be willing to heal when you don't believe you deserve it.

Lack of self-forgiveness creates this voice of self-hate that only knows how to take. It'll take your smile, your growth, your lessons, then blame you. It's not your fault. You could not have predicted why or that things would go this way. There's nothing wrong with you. Forgiving yourself is not penalizing yourself for mistakes you made, it's not claiming ownership for their mistakes.

Forgiving yourself is deciding not to live with guilt

from your choices. We are our biggest critics. Even when our intentions are good, we find ways to be hard on ourselves. This alone keeps us from making strides to forgive ourselves. One of the things that makes lack of self-forgiveness such a powerful enemy is that it works in all phases.

In the phase where you're mourning the end of the relationship, it finds reasons to make you adopt all sort of blame. We start crowning ourselves as the reason why it didn't work. We tell ourselves it's because we are unworthy, because we aren't enough, because we are unlovable instead of the fact they couldn't love us or the relationship just wasn't worth it. We tell ourselves, we are responsible for all the bad. We put magnifying glasses on our flaws and chastise ourselves for the obvious things that seemingly could've prevented our heartbreak. We cast blame on ourselves for things beyond our control.

When you're done mourning and moving forward, you are faced with a different angle of unforgiveness towards self. You start to analyze your mistakes and now blame yourself for your choices, questioning why you weren't careful enough, how you allow yourself to be fooled, why you believed in love again, why you missed the red flags.

You create a long laundry list of mistakes that can no longer be fixed. Self-forgiveness is important because of that. Because we don't realize how much we mistreat ourselves, are ungraceful towards ourselves, and hurt ourselves.

Forgiving yourself is allowing yourself to be human. We all make mistakes, we all land in positions we shouldn't be in, we've all been disappointed by something. Many fall for people and traps we shouldn't have. It's not all your fault; but for what was, acknowledge your error and move forward. Look in the mirror and tell yourself that your past mistakes aren't who you are. They are a part of you, the past you. They don't have to always be you.

When those negative thoughts start to rise is when you must remind yourself that people make mistakes. As long you are alive, you have time to do better. You will eventually get it right and love will come. Healing is not just about what was done to you by others. Healing from what you've done to yourself is equally as important.

The journey to self-forgiveness will come with a lot of reversing your thinking and rehearsing things you must do. Lots of people find results with writing, practicing affirmations, and even finding confirmation. I encourage you to pick up a journal (preferably one of my lovely journals) and write the good things you value about yourself. Write about the lessons you learned from your mistakes. Write yourself into a good light. Remind yourself of the times you tried your best, the times you loved your hardest and it wasn't reciprocated.

Even when you weren't the best friend, partner, or lover, you still gave it a shot. Find the positive in your negative, find the good and sit on it. It's okay to speak good things.

In the practical section of this book, you will find more applicable things to do along with the affirmation book created for this. You need to find a way to get this done in order to heal. It's one of the hardest things to do and one that has less focus. It impacts your self-love, self-confidence, self-esteem. Forgiving yourself has to be seen as something that isn't optional.

Clean that room for improvement.

We all have room for improvement, it's up to us to open the door to that room and start doing what it takes to make it happen. Healing is something that doesn't happen without improvements. Healing is not supposed to be just fixing or repairing what's been broken. It's about putting the pieces back in a way that makes it overall better than before.

It's not about just saying goodbye to the pain and the hurt but growing from it, learning from it. Countless times, I've heard people say, "I want to go back to who I was before them", "I want to get back to the old me."

Why? Who you were before them is the past. Now, you've got a handful of lessons and experience to build on. You must build on it. The entire journey of healing itself is about improving. There's no moving backwards in moving on. It's moving forward, this means moving away from the past that no longer serves you. Even if it's the old version of you.

The goal is to make sure you don't just let the scars

heal and return to what was once before. That's a waste of your experience. Evolving must come with healing, growth is part moving forward.

There's a huge opportunity to improve yourself when you are letting go and moving on. This is an opportunity many miss because they are stuck pointing fingers. It's always the ex's fault. It's always the ex who did the betraying, the disappointing, the hurting, and every-thing else bad. It's never our fault.

There has to be a self-evaluation. Once you forgive them and forgive yourself, the next step is looking into the mirror to find what you contributed to the failure of that last relationship. Do not allow your healing to be about just overcoming what they did to you. It's time to look deep in the mirror and make it about you, along with them.

There's so much hint in the experiences, it would be foolish not to point fingers at yourself to find what to let go of. This is the next step after forgiving yourself. Forgiving yourself must come first because you must get out of the blaming mindset to do this properly. This isn't about carrying blame but looking for areas to correct. One is for the purpose of change, the other puts a pause on change.

You have to spend time collecting lessons, searching for understanding, addressing deep things and doing your absolute best to walk away from this victorious. Maybe you finally see how you could've loved better. Maybe you see how much more you should've given to the relationship. Perhaps part of the way you communicated caused some tension. Your lack of self-control may have caused some mess. You could've been more affectionate, more understanding, more loving.

You are not exempt. You must be held accountable, as well, to get the full benefit of growing from the situation. There are things you didn't do that must be fixed and improved. You must reflect and grow.

Beware when you are looking at your faults and making the changes you needed to make, that they don't signal you back into a dead relationship. The lessons, most of the times, are for you to be better in the next relation-ship.

The reality is you making necessary improvements will not make your ex-partner better or your relationship better. Relationships worth resurrecting require growth all around, a similar level of dedication to changing. Cleaning your own room for improvement is about bettering yourself overall, becoming a more mature and aware lover. You cannot dwell in this phase; there's no good in tracing steps trying to right your wrongs when trying to move. Leave the chapter closed.

I became a better husband because of this exact process. In my self-evaluation after the last relationship before my marriage, I realized how guarded I was, how unaffectionate I could be at times. I had this fear of being heartbroken that destroyed my last relationship.

When I met my wife, I made sure I wasn't going to repeat my mistake. I forced myself to be affectionate. I told myself I was going to make my whole heart fair game, not just part of it. When I started dating my wife, I opened my soft side. I started holding hands and hugging in public not giving a care if we were seen.

Before, I was always afraid of doing certain things because I grew to dislike them or thought there was something wrong with them. Like PDA. I didn't like it and it also made more people aware of our relationship. I never wanted to be associated with a partner so when it didn't work out, not many people knew. I broke free from the worries that came with the fear of being heartbroken. I allowed myself to love and be loved without putting up a bunch of unnecessary walls.

I came into my current relationship with so much improvement and it worked. This is how I ended up marrying my wife. I had become a much better lover. The corrections I made allowed me to freely love my wife, build strong trust and loyalty simply because the fear did not have as much power over me. I made sure not to leave those blinders on after looking in the mirror.

The difference between this relationship and my last is almost black and white. I've grown to trust this woman to a level I've never trusted anyone. A lot of my guards are down which helps us have healthy conversations and grow with one another.

Looking in the mirror and making changes is important for your healing. It's not about looking to see where they hurt you in order to heal. It's about looking to

see where you hurt others and where you hurt yourself.
Growth doesn't come without correction. You need to be
corrected of some things. It's time for you to search deep
and look for what has to go and what needs to come in.

Practical Things To Do

When you understand what you are going through
and how to handle it, the next step is doing the
action steps. Knowledge without execution
is of almost no value.

Developing the right mindset and having the proper outlook on things is only half of the battle. With understanding, you need to take proper steps to move on. We've discussed the right foundation, now we must lay the bricks.

To execute, it will take doing things you are not comfortable with, things that will challenge you. It will require discipline, consistency, and honesty. This is where effort comes in. This is where the sweat and tears will produce the results you desire.

Disconnect and change focus.

You don't need to be in contact with your ex whatsoever, unless you have children with them you need to communicate about. You need to get disconnected, unfollow them, delete the text thread, block the number, etc. You need to do whatever it takes to detach yourself from them.

Before we dive into this, you must prioritize why you are doing this. We've already discussed how 'out of sight, out of mind' doesn't bring healing. So, this is not what getting disconnected is about. Getting disconnected is about not putting your emotions in jeopardy once again. It's about setting boundaries that will help you reach your goal. It's doing what's necessary to put the past in the past.

Everyone finds it easy to block their ex. It's a reaction to the emotions, a way to handle the pain. What is not easy is making sure you don't find yourself snooping around, doing things to keep some type of connection. Disconnecting for the right reason requires you to be disciplined and committed.

If you're not one of the people who is disconnected out of sheer emotions and anger, please listen to me: you are not a loser if you are doing this. You are not weaker; this isn't testing your self-control or will power. This is about putting a plan forward to keep you emotionally stable, growing, and burying the past.

You are not doing yourself a favor trying to be strong enough to go against the urge to communicate with them. This is running away from the temptation, not embracing a false sense of maturity.

You had feelings for this person. If you do not pull yourself away, you will slowly get sucked into something that is dead or should be dead. Something that you don't need to be in. You have to do this to have fewer distractions as you move forward. Temptation always finds the best victims in those who think they can withstand it. You will feed right into it trying to beat it.

Now, how do you disconnect and focus?

There's no formula to this. There are practices you can

apply.

Practice utilizing the bad thoughts to your advantage. When you feel like contacting your ex, you must convince yourself not to. There's absolutely no need to be in contact with them. You must keep your thoughts focused on that.

Speak to yourself about why you deserve better. Remind yourself of bad times. Think about the negative impact this breakup had in your life. Focus on the bad that the relationship brought to your life. You have to mentally trick yourself into seeing the issue with communicating with them. When you put the experience in the worst light or for many, realistic lights, it keeps you from wanting to have anything to do with that.

Practice staying away from triggers. You will run into things that trigger you; things that will shoot down your progress if you allow them. You must learn to identify them and eliminate them quickly. You must keep yourself away from the things that can influence your mind, your memories, and your emotions.

Flee from them quickly, or they can slowly draw you to start entertaining what you shouldn't. Be aggressive with some of these if you have to. The goal is to protect your current growth. Eventually, those triggers will no longer be triggers. While they are, you must keep them from triggering.

Monitor yourself to see what affects you differently and how they pull you back to those old thoughts or habits. It's vital to cut them quickly.

Below is a list of common triggers I've observed that creep up on us the most.

➤ *Trigger: Entertainments*

Certain songs, TV shows, movies, actors, and even singers that will trigger you. During the time of the relationship, you built some memories together. Those memories attach themselves to different things, entertainment is an easy one.

Remember that one song you sung together? That one movie you both cried to? That one Netflix show you both binge watched or were still waiting on the new season of? Those can be distractions.

When you find yourself enjoying those songs, movies, and shows make sure you monitor yourself ready to hit 'stop' if you need to. I don't want to make you do everything to avoid them, but you must put boundaries that don't pull you back.

I stopped listening to "I Won't Give Up on You" by Jason Mraz simply because it was the theme song for one of my exes and I. Although I loved the song, it kept putting me in a state of mind that made me miss her. And, in some cases, tempt me to reach out. If I am being completely honest, I even reached out to her once before because of it. I had to stay away from the song until the memories attached no longer had an effect on me. It gradually went from 'this is our song' to 'this used to be our song' to 'I just love this song.' Limit yourself; without discipline results are hard to come by.

➤ *Trigger: Friendships*

There are friendships you will need to stay away

from to keep your focus. Friendships that were formed by the relationship are usually the main ones. Lots of times, those friendships dissolve. If yours didn't, you will need to set boundaries that keep them from distracting you. If they talk too much about your ex and it's triggering you, you have to do something.

You may need to ask them not to do it in your presence or you can take the initiative to stay away from their presence. Something must be done. If there's no disconnecting that can come from certain friendships, you might want to enjoy the friendship from a distance. This is not about being extreme if you're thinking that. It's about having tunnel vision. The friendships you pause will probably no longer become triggers when you've really moved on.

Right at this moment, if it's not helping you, you must cut it. Of course, you shouldn't cold turkey the whole thing or do it without communication. Believe it or not, most people who care for you want to help you do what's best for you. Don't be afraid to do what needs to be done.

➤ *Trigger: Content*

You must monitor what you consume during your healing journey, mostly what you consume online. Yes, it goes that deep. Are you watching a bunch of romantic movies? Following a bunch of "relationship goals" pages. Keeping your eyes on 'it' couples? How do those things make you feel? For me and many others, when we get involved in those things, we crave our exes. When we crave them, we go back to the closest memory of them. This is where distractions come in.

You start to either fall into regret, onboarding an emotional battle, or you listen to your cravings and go to the nearest person you can get that from. The type of content people consume alone can be responsible for them falling into rebound relationships or running back to revive the dead ones.

As a poet and author, lots of people follow me and consume my content to heal from broken relationships, some to build their self-love, some to build better relationships. The same applies; consume what will help you. Just like there's content out there that will help you, there's also content that will hurt you or distract you. Be wise with what you follow, listen to, and watch.

Practice unplugging. The toughest part about disconnecting is the timing. Pull the plug quickly on anything reconnecting you to what you are letting go of. You must learn to act quickly on burning down the distractions.

If you're on Instagram and you have the urge to unblock them and stalk, LOG OFF Instagram. If you're getting texts from them, maybe they are using a different number... don't wonder, BLOCK THEM. If you have the urge to text them yourself, put your phone away and go do something else or find one of the things that I've listed here to distract you. You have to practice unplugging quickly. Learning to nip whatever is coming to take you off your path quickly can be life changing.

Write and read.

You must feed both your mind and soul, as well as empty them to truly move on and heal. It's emptying your cup of the old and pouring in the new. The venting and learning process is a vital part of your healing process. There's no better way to do those than to write and read.

Let's talk about writing. Writing is very therapeutic. It's a perfect tool to emotionally drain yourself of all the bad things and also the perfect brain dump of anything. As a writer, I do it both to pour my creativity and pour my heart. Before becoming an official writer, I did it to vent, to reflect, to connect with my emotions, and to heal.

Writing is a beautiful and safe place to vent. Your thoughts have the opportunity to be private and secured. You get to say everything you want however you want, and nobody can repeat it back to you, nor do you have to limit how deep you express yourself.

As mentioned before, one of the most important things about writing is that it helps filter out the negative thoughts. Those thoughts bottled in only create a more toxic environment in your mind. Emptying these thoughts will prevent them from turning into more unproductive thoughts and building up worse scenarios and angles. It's necessary.

Find a journal to do all your writing. Physically do it. Pick up a pen or pencil and go to work. I created a journal specifically for this part because I want to make sure you have resources to do this. A journal has to be the main place this happens. Dumping your thoughts in the wrong places can be bad also. So head over to **pierrejeanty.com** to grab your journal and get to work.

The one place you don't need to do your writing is on social media. You don't need to vent there, welcoming everyone into your business and giving room for opinions you may not need. Society has become a place of no filters or boundaries, with the help of social media. There can be good to that, but it often produces bad. People keep very little privacy, airing out all of their dirty laundry to people who have no business knowing intimate things about them. Don't open the door for people to have opinions about parts of your life they should earn the privilege to know.

Protect yourself by being private about your issues during these times. Keep it offline.

There is the case where you can use it to write poetry like I did. I took what I felt and polished it up to create a message for others rather than vent. I never share dirty laundry; instead, I air my experiences in a professional way. That is the only way I recommend venting publicly. You can share the pain or the lesson with a purpose. Don't let it be anything more. Sharing on social media can also welcome distractions and even predators who may be looking to capitalize off your pain. Write your heart out, but for you.

What should you write about?

Write about everything. What you write can help you process different things. Writing about how you met or the things you loved in the beginning can help you process the memories. Writing about the things you've learned, appreciated, and love can help you identify what to grow from. Writing about when it all started to the end, how it felt, and what went wrong can help you put the relationship behind. Write about everything.

- Write about the first impression they made on you.

- Write about when you first fell in love with them.

- Write about when you realized you were falling out of love.

- Write about what you appreciated about them the most.

- Write about the disagreement that started shifting things.

- Write about what you put up with and shouldn't have.

- Write about the red flags you purposely ignored.

Write. Write. Write. I have more prompts for you to empty out even the deepest negative things on paper. Once again, head over to **pierrejeanty.com** to get yours.

Let's talk about the reading.

Reading is one of the most important ways to download information and gain knowledge. You are doing it right now and it's helping you. Reading books, blogs, posts online, and other material to help you welcome new perspectives on how to deal with your current situation is needed.

Sometimes you may read and not find new insights to make a significant change. Even then, it may confirm some of your thought processes which could be all you needed. Reading helps you walk better on your path to healing or helps you stay on the path. Despite what the information is... READ. However, it speaks to you is not the point here, the point is to do it. If you do read, it will do something to you.

It's imperative that you test the information you are reading. When I say to just read, I don't mean to consume any type of material. It's important to make sure what you are reading is seasoned with wisdom and truth. It needs facts as well, but the thing with emotions is they often deal with truth. Everything I say may not be a fact to you, but you may find them to be true.

There are a lot of people giving bad advice on social media or in their books. There are a lot of well marketed blogs leading people down the wrong paths, helping them stay in their trap.

Once, I saw a writer who preached brokenness as a phase you must stay in and find the beauty in. This is crippling. While there can be beauty extracted from brokenness, it's not meant to be a stage you find comfort in. You must grow. This book is about not staying in that brokenness but actively working to get away from it.

Remember, it's easy for anybody to gain a platform and say things that agree with your negative feelings. One of our downfalls is that we love clinging to what is relatable more than we are to healing. Healing takes work, relating takes nothing. You don't need to read anything to validate your negative emotions. You don't need a blog about 'why breaking their windows is justifiable' or 'cheating with their best friend is good revenge'. Sounds absurd, but when people are dealing with break-ups, emotions can push them to do the unthinkable. People even kill over heartbreak. Be careful what you read. It should help you fight your demons, not enable them.

Write your heart out, it'll help you breathe better, it'll help you find your smile, it'll bring you some peace. Get those thoughts out. Feed your mind with resourceful information, this will help you guide your heart better. It will help transform you into the healed person you are trying to become.

Spend quality time with yourself.

When you are letting go, spending time with yourself will be easy. We all hibernate when we are heartbroken. When you are trying to heal, you will have to do the same thing with a different focus. This version of spending time alone in your own presence is not for the purpose of evaluating and thinking deeply. This is to practice self-care. You will be changing, evolving, becoming someone new, you need to get to know that person. You need to know your new likes and dislikes; what you enjoy or don't enjoy anymore. You will need to get in tune with the person you are becoming. This is where spending time with yourself becomes vital, it will help you get to know yourself more.

Take yourself out to lunch or dinner. Go to the movies with yourself. Attend an event with a party of one. Put an emphasis on doing something by yourself. I was speaking to someone about moving on once. One of the things they realized after their relationship was, not only did they refuse to eat by themselves, they felt bad about it.

They were used to showing up to a restaurant with more than a party of one. They had to get comfortable saying, "No it's only me eating."

You may need to do that. Try doing something you haven't done alone. The purpose of this is to explore you. A side benefit is it can lead to unexpected relationships forming, like new friendships. However, the primary focus is you being in your own presence and enjoying things for you. In this you will find the time to listen to yourself, recognize your needs, your wants, things you may have missed out on before because you were too busy living with someone else or for someone else.

Everything is fast nowadays; most people are too busy. This is almost a must when trying to move on because you need that special attention to add to your self-love and self-care tanks. Find the time to be all about you without being self-centered.

In my e-book, *"How to be Happy While Single: Choosing to be Content,"* I talk about dating yourself which is another thing you should do during this alone time phase. It helps build the self-awareness and confidence you need as you are moving forward.

In conclusion, spend time with yourself. You're consistently moving and consistently scrolling or being in the midst of people. Learn to put that down and exist without all that. You deserve your own attention, you deserve your own love, you deserve your own time. Give that to yourself.

Accept helping hands.

One of the things that will help you accelerate the process of moving on, is accepting helping hands. What we are dealing with is personal, we like to deal with it in private. I recommend you do so; but, there's also another side of this. A side where you accept outside help.

Get professional help if necessary

Sometimes, what you need is a therapist, coach, counselor, someone who will listen and help you reach deep into your thoughts and emotions to help bring you clarity. Someone who has a better understanding than the people you know and can provide professional help.

As someone who's done relationship coaching, I can honestly say it helps. I've seen clients go from their mind being fogged up and emotionally messy to having clarity, feeling more confident and at peace with their choices.

Perhaps you need more than guidance and confirmation. Maybe the heartbreak added some real deep scars where it left deep trauma, affected your mental health beyond sadness, or put you in a suicidal state. A mental health professional or licensed therapist may be the right person to reach out to.

First, there's nothing wrong with reaching out for help, we all need it. Second, don't be ashamed of the level where you are. We are all at different levels. Needing therapy or reaching out to the suicide prevention line doesn't make you less than. It means you need a different type of help.

We all can use some help navigating through the storm. There's no need to be embarrassed or any of that. There's nothing wrong with help. We all need help with something in our lives. Confidently take this step if you need it.

Accountability partner

Get connected with someone you can call when you are emotionally weak, when you are breaking down, or have the urge to make choices that go against your progress. An accountability partner is perfectly okay. They can be your professional help provider, a friend or family member who knows your goal and is there to motivate you to stick to it. They are like a personal trainer, your moving on coach (that's a new title, LOL). This is someone you call when you feel like running back to that unhealthy relationship, when you feel like responding to that 'I miss you' text or simply feel like welcoming your ex back in. Anytime you feel like breaking, you have this person to reach out to and they'll keep you on track. An accountability partner just keeps you 'accountable'.

The thing you must make sure of is that your accountability partner is someone wise, disciplined, and is a positive influence. They have to be mature enough to give you solid advice, to speak life into you and reason with you when you are making u-turns. They have to be someone who will not back down when you refuse to stick to your plan. A 'yes man' can't be an accountability partner. More than enough times that partner will have to tell you 'no.' That's their job, to keep you on track.

Now to make this effective, you must come to some terms. I don't want to make this simpler than it is. You must set a plan and both agree on it for it to work. Maybe you need to call them once a week. Maybe you need to tell them one thing that almost made you fall off track. You have to report something and expect feedback.

Often, this doesn't work for people because they start off good, then start sharing less or communicating less with their accountability partner. When the urges and desires rise and they really want to give into them without facing any resistance, they don't follow up with their partner. This is why you must put a plan in place to create some consistency. You must find something you can stick to.

Affirmations.

You've heard the term 'fake it 'til you make it.' For many this means faking for the purpose of fooling and for some it means acting as if it has already happened while doing everything to make it happen.

Affirmations are one of the best ways to fake it 'til you make it. It's also one of the best ways to renew your mindset. Our belief system is one of the most powerful tools we have. If we don't believe certain things, they just simply don't happen in our lives. If you don't believe you deserve forgiveness, you won't accept it. If you don't believe in love, you'll never find it. Whatever you don't believe in, usually won't happen.

That's why faking it works to a certain extent, because it makes you believe which is often the fuel for things to become a reality. This is where affirmations come in.

Affirmations will help you believe. Affirmations will help you rewire your thought process. Affirmations are positive words or statements that can help you confront the negative thoughts you face. They are words you can speak about yourself, that you will start to believe by repeating them enough. Affirmations are a tool to combat the negative beliefs with new ones that can help you make the positive and desired changes. To get to your healing, you need to believe the right things about yourself, the right things about your identity, what you deserve, what you need, and what you will become. Affirmations are the tool for that.

Here's a short list of affirmations that you may need to add to your routines.

I am worthy of true love.
I did not deserve the wrongs they committed unto me.

My heart does not have room for bitterness, envy, and forgiveness.

I forgive myself for...
I am more than my past mistakes.

I created an affirmation book to go well with this book to help you speak the right things about yourself. The simple words like the ones above are powerful and can make a world of a difference if you speak them. Now, you will need to get over the fact that you are talking to yourself when doing them, and your reality will say different. As long you stick to them, you will see some change. Learning to believe the right things about yourself will take time when you've been stuck on the bad things.

Another important thing is that different phases of your healing may require different affirmations. One of the things I took my time to do is make sure I created affirmations for every stage of this journey. I highly recommend you pick up a copy and follow along the way I've laid it out. Let's get you speaking and writing out the right things.

Conclusion

Congratulations, you've reached the end of this book. You've made it! You read all the way through to here. I am proud of you. I am glad that you've pushed yourself to get this far. You and I know this is just the beginning. The beginning of your process, of your growth, your healing.

Moving on is serious business; it's something you must prepare for. Something you need to put real effort and real time into. It takes real commitment. You understand, this puts you ahead of so many people who are practicing so many of the things we covered. You see the value, you are equipped now. Let's get going into the right direction. Let's get you healed and ready for the relationship that will last.

I beg you to not just appreciate this book but to put everything you've read to use. I challenge you to practice the things I've suggested and become dedicated to your progress. I challenge you to do the boring things, the things you don't feel like doing, the hard things because they will be what become the vehicle to get you where you need to be.

You will feel like giving up on this journey; you will feel like it's too much. I want to remind you that it's not. There's no need to waste your pain, waste your experience, waste more time. You've got your uniform on soldier, it's time to do what it takes to win your heart, mind, and soul back.

Don't ever think the fact that you feel stuck sometimes is weakness. Don't ever think seeking help is too much, don't ever settle. Most importantly, don't ever think your pace is too slow. Just keep on marching, keep on applying yourself, keep on going. Moving on is not a fast process; it takes time, though the healing part doesn't just come with time.

I hope these words bring some clarity to make this journey easier for you. A happy, healed, and better you is waiting for you to come claim it. This is just a pit stop until you reach the end of the tunnel and fall into new light. You are equipped for your destination. Go after it. You deserve freedom, you deserve closure, you deserve better.

Lastly, I want to offer more to you, to serve you

REALLY MOVING ON 167

beyond just sharing my thoughts. After writing this book, I created a list of things that will help you do the leg work. I created an affirmation book to help you replace the bad thoughts and mindsets. I created a journal to help pour your heart out. I created a membership program to help you have a sense of community and not walk this path alone. I created a course to help you do a deeper dive and tackle the things that aren't covered here along with a workbook.

I want you to win. You are more than welcome to allow me to pour into your journey directly. I even opened my text message inbox to get your feedback and answer different questions when I can. Text "MoveOn" to (239) 203-2991 to be a part of that. I am here for you on this journey. I want you to put everything behind you and love in front of you.

ABOUT THE AUTHOR

Pierre Alex Jeanty, most widely known for his international best sellers *HER* & *HER Vol.2*, is a Haitian-American author, publisher, life coach, and entrepreneur. Often approached for relationship advice and dealing with the same issues himself, Pierre found a passion for writing on the topics of dating, love, and relationships. After leaving his 9-to-5 in 2014 to become a full-time relationship blogger, Pierre released his first book *Unspoken Feelings of a Gentleman* which quickly rocketed to success.

Since then, he's maintained a balance between writing self-help and writing poetry. He also writes for men and women, which led to him to launch the HER series in 2017. Pierre's focus is to share his own love journey and lessons from his past, with the hope that it inspires men to become better, and to be a voice of hope to women who have lost faith in good men.

Pierre currently resides with his family in southwest Florida where he operates as the founder of Jeanius Publishing, a publishing company dedicated to helping authors. Pierre also occasionally travels as a speaker and is the host of "The REALationship Therapy" podcast with his wife, Natalie Jeanty.

You can connect with Pierre on these platforms:

@Pierrejeanty

Pierre Alex Jeanty

@PierreAJeanty

Email – contact@jeaniuspublishing.com

Other books by Pierre

Best Sellers
HER.
HER Vol. 2
Ashes of Her Love
Unspoken Feelings of a Gentleman
To the Women I Once Loved
Apologies That Never Came

Other Books
Her. Guided Journal
Unspoken Feelings of a Gentleman 2
In Love With You
Heal. Grow. Love.
Sparking her own Flame
Watering Your Soil

Free Downloads
Watering Your Soil
Download at www.wateringyoursoil.com

RESOURCES

reallymovingon.com/membership

reallymovingon.com/community

reallymovingon.com/masterclass

reallymovingon.com/affirmations